ROAD TO RECOVERY

Pathways to Spirituality

PERSONAL STORIES BY PEOPLE WHO'VE BEEN THERE

EDITED BY DALE H.

FOREWORD BY DR. ROBERT J. ACKERMAN

PUBLISHED BY THE RENASCENT FOUNDATION

Copyright

Pathways to Spirituality

Copyright © 2015 Renascent Foundation Inc.

Library and Archives Canada Cataloguing in Publication

Pathways to Spirituality / edited by Dale H.

Issued in print and electronic formats.

ISBN 978-0-9947998-4-5 (paperback).--ISBN 978-0-9947998-5-2 (ebook)

1. Alcoholics--Rehabilitation. 2. Recovering alcoholics--Religious life.

I. H., Dale, 1957-, editor

HV5278.P38 2015   616.86'106   C2015-904949-0

C2015-904950-4

Cover by Jacques Pilon Design Communications

Print format by Chris G.

Published by Renascent Foundation Inc.

Dedication

This is book is dedicated to...

the thousands of men, women and children who've found recovery through Renascent. Your recovery stories let others know that recovery is possible and beautiful — even in the face of challenges that once may have seemed insurmountable.

our Guardian Angels and all of our donors, small and large — who support recovery by making charitable gifts to the Renascent Foundation. With donors by our side, cost is removed as a barrier for the majority who seek help but cannot afford to pay.

Acknowledgements

Editor: Dale H.

Publishing Facilitator: Roger C.

Editorial Committee: Anne P., Caroline L., Dale H., Jeff C., Petra M., Roger C.

Proofreader: Christine Sanger

Renascent Foundation Project Manager: Joanne Steel

Published by Renascent Foundation Inc.
Lillian and Don Wright Family Health Centre
38 Isabella Street, Toronto, ON M4Y 1N1
Charitable #11911 5434 RR0001

24/7 Recovery Helpline: 1-866-232-1212

www.renascent.ca

Table of Contents

Foreword

You have a right to recovery. You have a right to achieve recovery anyway you can. There are numerous paths to recovery and there are numerous paths to spirituality. For many, spirituality is a major source and part of their recovery. You also have the right to define spirituality anyway you want. For some, it is a belief in the human spirit. For others, it is a sense of spirituality. For still others, it is a belief in a higher power. For some, it is a belief in God. For others, it is a belief in you. The common denominator is having a belief.

I am well aware of the controversy of a belief in God as it relates to 12-step programs. This dilemma usually occurs when it is believed that the Higher Power of the program must mean God. I am also aware that you have the right to define a Higher Power anyway you want. I believe that no one has the right to tell another person what to believe. However, there are many people who want to share what has worked for them on their journey to recovery. The authors of the stories in this book share what has worked for them. There is a high probability that since you are reading this book, you share many of their beliefs; however, you might not. Both viewpoints are acceptable, aren't they?

Often, when people seek recovery, they are not sure what they believe. Often, they are searching for something that will provide meaning for their lives and a sense of direction for the future. I believe that no one recovers by themselves. Somewhere, somehow, influences outside of us begin to impact our recovery.

I was raised in foster care from birth. Most of the time it was okay, but there were times of physical abuse and in one case it was very severe. I remember being held against a wall while a man held a shotgun that he aimed at me and threatened to pull the trigger. I remember being beaten to the point of not being able to get up. When I was six years old, I was adopted and finally I had parents; however, within four years, my father developed alcoholism. Throughout all of this and many difficult situations that followed, I always believed that I was not alone. I believed that someone was

1

looking out for me. I believed that my life would get better and I believed that I was given the ability to make it better. And, since I was not alone, it was going to happen. This belief was and has been the most powerful influence in my life. For me, this is spirituality. Erik Erickson believed that the greatest crime of humanity is to destroy the spirit of a child. Fortunately for me, mine was not.

Spirituality is very personal. It deserves respect, not debate. In the 12-step recovering community, it is the belief that makes the program work. Recovery often provides a sense of well-being or a sense of contentment with our lives. This comes from spirituality. This comes from believing that we are not alone.

Dr. Robert J. Ackerman

Bluffton, SC

USA

Introduction

My name is Dale and I am an alcoholic.

Twenty years ago, I said these words to a roomful of women in Walker House, Renascent's treatment centre for women at that time. I certainly didn't want to be there. But somewhere under the fog of my alcoholism, at my very bottom, I knew that I needed to be there. I had nowhere else to go.

Over the next 28 days, I would say those same words again and again. I would listen as the other women shared their pain, their fear, their anger, their shame and confusion. I would learn just what alcoholism was and why I could not drink "normally." Most importantly, I would learn that there was a solution, that there was hope, that recovery was indeed possible. Renascent has continued to be a touchstone in my personal journey of recovery throughout the years. I can never repay what they so freely and lovingly gave me.

Ten years ago, I was asked to guest edit a few issues of the Renascent alumni newsletter, TGIF Weekly Recovery News. Little did I know that today I'd be looking back on a decade of work as the newsletter's editor and have the joy of seeing the writers' contributions evolve into an anthology series of print and e-books.

TGIF was created in 2000 by Renascent Alumni Coordinator Lisa North as an innovative means of strengthening and supporting our far-flung alumni community by using the then rather cutting-edge technology of email and web browsers. In keeping with the 12-step tradition of storytelling, the newsletter (initially named tiktalk) largely consisted of Lisa's weekly reflections on recovery, supplemented by announcements of alumni events and sobriety anniversaries. The newsletter slowly evolved to contain interviews, relevant news stories and the occasional personal essay written by Renascent alumni, and was renamed TGIF.

Under the helm of Alumni Coordinator Charles McMulkin, TGIF evolved into an engaging, relevant and topical newsletter featuring lived experience essays written by Renascent alumni, coupled with contributions by professionals in the addiction and recovery field. During Joanne Steel's tenure, the voices of family members were strengthened and friends in the broader recovery community were invited to contribute their personal stories of recovery as well.

The juxtaposition of the didactic and the personal continues to be the foundation of TGIF. Videos, book reviews, poetry, special issues and Renascent outreach initiatives have all been added. But the heart of TGIF remains the personal stories told by alumni and others in recovery, from the newly sober to the long-timer.

Today, TGIF Weekly Recovery News reaches thousands of subscribers each week via email. All content also resides in our TGIF blog on the Renascent website (www.renascent.ca). Go have a look. There are over 1,000 articles and essays on just about any aspect of recovery you can imagine. Subscribe to TGIF while you're there!

As the editor of TGIF, I have long believed that these beautiful stories of recovery deserved a broader platform. Enter Joanne Steel, Renascent's Manager of Major Gifts and Communications. With Joanne's customary drive, passion and tenacity, these anthologies finally turned from dream into reality. Our volunteer editorial committee members spent hours poring through essays, looking to find the gems that best represent the limitless opportunities for growth offered to us as we live and learn in recovery.

The book you're holding features the experience, strength and hope of men and women who are living the reality of recovery each and every day. To them, we give our deepest thanks for their honesty and willingness to share their stories, their challenges and their victories as they walk the road of recovery with courage.

The "God question" has often presented a challenge to newcomers to 12-step recovery. Program literature makes it clear that the road to a spiritual awakening is a broad one, yet this essential truth can somehow get lost in translation. This volume reflects the experience of our writers: that spirituality can be experienced in any number of different ways.

You'll read stories of people of different religious faiths or none at all, atheists, agnostics, those who embrace other spiritual traditions, those who find their higher power in a higher purpose or through their creative spirit. All these voices and more are a chorus of hope and encouragement that you too can tap into "an unsuspected inner resource" on your own journey of recovery.

Essays written by Renascent alumni indicate the Renascent house they attended and the year they went through treatment. Contributions by our friends in the broader recovery community are identified by name alone. Renascent uses the 12-step treatment model (in conjunction with other treatment modalities) and, in accordance with the tradition of anonymity, all writers are identified by first name and last initial only.

Finding a Higher Power

Doug Rudolph

From the purest religious faith to new-age atheism, when it comes to the Twelve Steps, the concept of a Higher Power has served it all. For some people, "faith" comes easy. But for many others, finding a Higher Power can be a painstaking and difficult process — which can feel defeating at times.

The simple truth is that what we actually believe isn't important. What matters is awakening that inner part of the "human spirit" that connects us to other people, to the world, and to a sense of purpose, meaning, hope, and strength to move forward on our sober journey. Exactly what we think we're connecting to, or how we go about it, is not as important as how we use that connection, how we live our lives and how we relate to things outside of ourselves. In other words, a Higher Power can help us realize that what we do matters — to ourselves, to the people we care about and to the world.

Following is our list, in no particular order, of the top five Higher Powers used by people in 12-step recovery. Our goal is to capture the basic essence of each Higher Power to illustrate how and why people find them effective, and to give people who may be struggling something to work with.

1. Music

Music has long been said to be the language of love. But to many, it's much, much more. In a way, music resonates everything we are, we were and we hope to be — it's the "spirit of life" in sound. Countless addicts (and people in general) have been "saved" by simply relating to the words in a song.

For many, music is the only thing that really gets through. Whether people are playing it or simply listening to it, music has the unique power to speak to people even when they shut out the world. It's not only a means of expression; rather, it's a salvation.

A soothing sound can cleanse people's deepest emotions or help them cope with a painful experience. A song can give people hope or help them find meaning in something they don't understand. Music can be a comforting voice. Lyrics can see people through a difficult time by them just being able to relate to the struggle. Music can be a sort of melodic counsellor or therapist, helping people find insight and strength to persevere.

In other words, music so often describes what we need but can't put into words. By doing so, it has a peculiar way of evoking in us a greater comprehension of life. As a Higher Power, for many, music is the sound of spirituality, which not only enhances the human experience, but serves as a connection to the very rhythm of our existence.

2. Nature

In all of Nature's beauty yet unforgiving wrath, what an awe-inspiring force it is. From watching the sun set to lying on a moonlit beach, connecting with Mother Nature can liberate the soul. For many people, Nature is God. It's the Grand Architect; the all-powerful creator and provider of life.

Some people favour empirical study and discovery as ways of relating to Nature, while others choose a more mystical path, preferring direct experience through action, art, meditation and other methods.

For Nature's followers, the circle of life is an essential cornerstone of a beautiful, transformative process, which is not to be taken for granted. Just as a tree grows or a flower blooms, to them, human life is meant to flourish — to evolve, thrive, and be explored and experienced to the fullest in all its forms. In other words, Nature is hope.

As a Higher Power, the transcendental mind of Mother Nature serves as the ultimate source of guidance and inspiration — and Nature's will commands the betterment of the earth and all the life that lives here. Nature is love and the very soil of our existence, which lays fertile ground for salvation when awakened to its spirit.

3. The Universe

The cosmos: it captures both the imagination and the very nature of our existence. For many, the universe symbolizes not only all we are, but also all that we could become. Aligning oneself with the rhythm and fabric of the universe is the very essence of spirituality.

For many, energy equals action in which choices have consequences. Many people believe that simply doing "the next right thing" can set in motion a quantum chain of events in which the universe "rewards" positive choices. Some people look for messages, while others see it as a sort of karma. But they all believe they're a source of energy on an infinite journey. Faith is not only a quest for understanding, it's an insatiable drive "to know." Yet it's not always about finding an answer — the mystery is salvation.

The universe is a force beyond our comprehension, which captivates and intrigues. For many, simply imagining the possibilities can free the mind from the shackles of obsession, and give strength from the unknown. Our tiny existence amid an infinite space is the ultimate source of humility. Yet knowing that the entire space-time continuum has led to this very moment — and to you, as many believe — can invigorate and inspire a personal sense of limitless potential.

4. Humanity

People have a unique way of bringing out the best in each other, even when we appear to be at our worst. Humanity is an interconnected network of human life in all its forms — and for many, nurturing its "spirit" is the path toward salvation. Many people believe that life is a force which by its very nature commands it be nurtured and lived. From raising families to building societies to our sense of culture and community to simply hanging out with friends, people thrive by interacting with one another and the world in which we live.

And many people find strength in focusing on the positive attributes of others. To them, human virtue is the essence of our existence, and connecting to others and the world is the ultimate source of spiritual support. Faith in humanity is compassion, and understanding that even when we're alone, we're in this together.

For many, through practicing kindness, generosity, humility and honesty, humanity points them toward the right action — which is not to say they never mess up. Faith in humanity is about people knowing their limitations, while striving for growth. It's about people embracing their faults, while learning from their mistakes. For many, faith in humanity is about helping to ease others' suffering without always having the answer — it's just showing up for the call.

In other words, faith in humanity is about tapping into the best of which we are capable — because hidden behind every hardship, there's hope. And there's power in our ability to relate to each other, as many believe, because there's a little bit of each of us in us all.

5. The Faceless, Nameless God

Last but certainly not least, not everyone needs to define his or her Higher Power. For many, "knowing" is not an issue — the important thing is knowing they're not alone. Their Higher Power is an unseen and indescribable force that is the very sustenance of life. It's the soul of spirituality, which connects everyone and everything — and that's all they need to know.

When they struggle, it's a shoulder to lean on, which gives them strength — their Higher Power is unconditional support, which demands nothing in return. When they feel on top of the world, it keeps them in check — their Higher Power is the baseline between extremes; it's balance.

Whether it's Nature, humanity, music, the universe, a little of each, or something else entirely, to many, belief in a Higher Power is about getting out of themselves and knowing that it's okay to need help. It's just a matter of letting go of that control, especially when they start to fall. Faith gives them personal resolve to get back up on their feet. They may not know exactly what their Higher Power is, but it's clearly defined in their lives. Through their actions and words, and the way they interact with the world, their lives are a testament to its truth.

In other words, by defying explanation, their Higher Power has a strange way of giving meaning to all their questions — yet the answer is not what they seek. It's faith in knowing that when they're lost, their Higher Power is the direction that points them toward salvation.

Doug Rudolph is a leading recovery advocate in the United States. He's the Chief Policy Officer for and a founding member of Young People in Recovery (http://inrecovery.co/), a U.S. national advocacy organization focused on expanding resources for young people in or seeking recovery. A vocal proponent of the many pathways to recovery, Doug also serves as YPR's resident lawyer-in-training, earning a Juris Doctor in 2015 from Western New England School of Law.

What Would [insert name] Do?

Jason A. (Sullivan 2006)

The visitor, neatly groomed and bright-eyed, smiled gently as his tall, craggy faced host reached for the bottle and offered him a drink.

"No, thanks," Ebby said. "I'm not drinking."

"Not drinking! Why not?" Bill was so surprised that he stopped pouring to look with concern at his old friend. "What's the matter?"

"I don't need it anymore," Ebby replied simply. "I've got religion."

Religion? Damn! For a fleeting moment, Bill wondered about his friend's sanity. Ebby, after all, was a drinking buddy from way back. Now, apparently, he had gone off the deep end — his alcoholic insanity had become religious insanity!

Bill gulped a slug of gin. Well, dammit, not him. Religion was for the weak, the old, the hopeless; he'd never "get religion."

This story, which I first read about in the first chapter of the Big Book of Alcoholics Anonymous, is one I could very easily identify with after my first exposure to AA around four years ago. Faced with the prospect of losing everything — my family, my home, and even my life — I looked at AA as a way of saving my "stuff."

What I found at my first meeting in a church basement was a couple of prayers and a half a dozen references to that "G" word, God. I immediately judged AA to be a religious organization that I wanted no part of. And just like Bill, I continued to drink.

Unfortunately, it took an entire year before I realized how wrong that initial judgment was!

Growing up, I had no bias for or against religion or God. I was raised in a home where it wasn't really talked about much. My parents aren't religious people, but I don't recall them ever saying anything against it. Somehow in my teenaged wisdom I came to my own conclusion that there couldn't be a God if bad things happened to

13

good people, as we see all the time in the newspapers and on television.

It was almost 20 years later before I learned that the principles that ensure recovery in Alcoholics Anonymous are also at the core of every spiritual philosophy or religious body, but exist in AA without the ritual or dogma of an organized religion.

The principles of the Twelve Steps are really about living with our own flawed humanity and in harmony with one another.

Honesty, Faith, Courage, Willingness, Humility, Brotherly Love, Service ... they all sound like such impossibly high standards to live up to, especially for someone like me who had become so selfish and self-centred — a liar, a cheat and a thief.

But when I really try to practice these ideas in my daily life, every day turns out to be a pretty good day.

I do not need to become a Catholic or a Muslim, attend services, or give offerings in order to experience peace in my life. I only have to try to apply these principles to my thoughts and actions.

And it's a good thing too, because what Bill's Story doesn't say is that his friend with the new-found religion went on to drink on and off for another 30 years and died destitute. Sadly, as I've come to see, simply declaring oneself to be "religious" is absolutely no guarantee of continuous sobriety.

Like most people's spiritual journey, mine has certainly not been perfect. And therein lies the beauty of it! When I look back at the mistakes I've made and the people I may have harmed — even after my last drink — I naturally have some regret, but it's not nearly as great as the gratitude I have for the lessons I've been taught.

The important thing for me is to accept the imperfections in my own life and in my spiritual practices as a sign of my own humanity.

In order to solve the drink problem and start making a better life for myself and the people around me, I had to give up the notion that I had the power to make things perfect.

Basically, I had to accept that I was not God, and that something else could be. I came up with a Higher Power, which is bigger than any words can describe, and is the only thing that can possibly have absolute honesty, purity, unselfishness and love.

Sometimes it helps to use a really simple approach when applying the spiritual principles in our daily affairs. Just ask yourself: "What would [Higher Power/Jesus/Gandhi/Dalai Lama/Mohammad/my sponsor] do in this situation?"

The answer usually comes down to acting with love and compassion, and that never fails to bring serenity to my life.

In the Fellowship of the Spirit

Máire O.

Seeking seems to have been a theme in my life for as far back as I can remember, so the Eleventh Step should not have been unfamiliar territory. The spiritual journey was not that unfamiliar, either. However, one may not have picked that up about me while watching me tear the heart and soul out of myself in search of gratification that could never be satisfied.

Drawn to the contemplatives of my faith tradition, I often found myself deeply engrossed in one book or another, trying to pick up by reading what the authors had attained through gruelling lives of self-sacrifice for the benefit of others. I could never get that far, of course, because I was trying to grasp that for which I was not willing to work.

And so the state of serenity I read about remained something of a mystery — one for saints and holy men and women, but not for the likes of this sodden alcoholic.

I didn't really put prayer and meditation together, either, though it seems rather logical. Prayer was either very public (upstairs in a church) or private ("as I lay me down to sleep") and usually meant wholeheartedly beseeching relief from yet one more intolerable situation that I had likely gotten myself into.

Meditation I often did under the influence of a mind-altering substance. I learned somewhere that I should ask in meditation (sounds like a prayer, doesn't it?) for the obstacles that kept me from realization of the great cosmic unconscious to be removed. Well, one day I walked into a meeting of Alcoholics Anonymous and realized that my request had been realized.

Through a ton of hard work on the Steps with my sponsor and being active in service, I have come to realize that our prayers are answered in a time not of our own; some say "in God's time."

I really think that as I worked the Steps, I was inherently searching for knowledge of my Higher Power's will for me and the power to carry that out. I needed to spend considerable time reflecting on how insane I became under the influence of alcohol and how deeply affected I was by the alcoholism in my family.

It is only with prayer and the reliance on my sponsor and the Fellowship that I have been able to deepen my understanding of, and therefore my relationship with, this Higher Power. It is well beyond anything I could ever have hoped for while "out there."

Arrogance, indifference, anger and greed had wreaked havoc all around me. As I cleared away the wreckage of the past, more was revealed about the many ways I purposely, though quite unconsciously, thrived behind self-constructed road blocks. Constant diligence and reliance on this Higher Power helped to bring down the barriers. For decades, I didn't even know they were there!

For years in sobriety, I resisted improving my conscious contact with this Higher Power through meditation. My introduction to Zen several years ago was a conversion experience. I found the silence I had been searching for outside myself all my life. Sitting still, counting my breaths, is so comforting, so simple.

It often takes time to get the mind to settle down enough to feel the silence, but it is time well spent. As my mind reviews the myriad thoughts that arise, I am conscious of things I need to lay down, those I need to pay attention to, and those that are none of my business.

As these thoughts settle down, I am blessed with moments of deep serenity. The world is a perfect place; there is not one thing that I would change if I could. It is a genuine gift. A litany of prayers seems to be redundant — asking for that which is already well taken care of.

I have a choice when I arise from the period of meditation — whether to carry on without the benefit of the graces that I tapped into moments ago or to carry them with me. I stumble a lot; I can easily forget about the gift and fall back into old, self-defeating behaviour.

If I am diligent about the meditation practice, however, it becomes easier to try a different way of behaving in practicing these principles in all my affairs. Thankfully, it is a lifetime practice of compassionate caring.

I couldn't do it alone and I am assured that I indeed am in the Fellowship of the Spirit, trudging along.

Something That Transcends Us

Roger C.

Is a higher power necessary in order to recover from alcoholism or addiction?

Twelve-step programs place a lot of importance on finding a higher power to get or to maintain a life free of drugs or alcohol. That has been the case ever since the Twelve Steps were first published in 1939 in the book, Alcoholics Anonymous. The Second Step talks of "a Power greater than ourselves" that can "restore us to sanity."

Some of the more non-religious members of AA and other 12-step fellowships object to the idea of a "Higher Power," arguing that it is just a placeholder for "God." Indeed, some of the acronyms for a higher power — Group Of Drunks or Good Orderly Direction — reinforce their suspicion. Certainly a higher power of some sort — which does not have to be a God — can be an invaluable tool in recovery.

My favourite quote about the higher power idea comes from cultural anthropologist Ernest Becker who wasn't even thinking about 12-step programs when he wrote in The Denial of Death:

> We always rely on something that transcends us, some system of ideas and powers in which we are embedded and which support us. This power is not always obvious. It need not be overtly a god...It can be the power of an all-absorbing activity, a passion, a dedication to a game, a way of life...

I was talking to my good buddy Wayne the other day. He is an alumni and addictions counsellor at Renascent with nine years plus of sobriety. I have a little over three years and we were yattering away passionately about what we need to do, one day at a time, in order not to pick up again. The most important thing for him, Wayne said, was "getting out of my head."

That sure rang a bell for me. There is a maze inside my head, sometimes a very dangerous one. I play hide-and-go-seek in there. I run up and down the stairs. I get resentful. I get bitter. I get angry. I dissect all the unfair things in my life. And then — I do it all over again. And there are mirrors, lots of them, inside my head, with little images representing just one thing — me in the past — and many of the images are broken. It is a maze that is all dead-ends.

Got to get out of there.

Isolation and self-obsession kills the addict or alcoholic.

We need an interest in something larger than ourselves, outside of ourselves, an "all-absorbing activity," as Becker put it. A preoccupation, a "passion," something that takes us outside of ourselves.

We need a higher power.

So, what might that power be? One suggestion is contained in the last of the Twelve Steps: service. What could get us out of our own heads more quickly than thinking about other people and their needs? Serving others is a direct way for an isolated and self-absorbed human being to begin restoring some balance, some "sanity," in his or her life.

My friend Wayne will no doubt tell you that he worked at Renascent first and foremost to maintain his own sobriety. Service gives us something that transcends us and supports us and lets us get out of our heads. We have all the choices in the world when it comes to our higher power.

It can be God. It can be service. It can be, as Becker wrote, "an all-absorbing activity, a passion, a dedication to a game, a way of life..."

And, to come back to our question at the beginning, is a higher power necessary in order to recover from alcoholism or addiction?

Two things for sure: First, in my own case, without something to get me out of my head, with its maze and mirrors and inevitable dead ends, I would be at serious risk of going back out again. And second, this "system of ideas and powers" must be of our own understanding for it to deliver that essential reprieve.

And all of that is from the Twelve Steps — especially the Second Step — which suggests "a Power greater than ourselves" can be a crucial asset in finding a way to "restore us to sanity" and move on from the horrors of alcoholism and addiction.

It's All About Connecting

Wylaine L. (Munro 2012)

"Do it to me, baby."

That's what I say to my higher power every morning. It's my personal, some may say freakish, way of saying "Thy will, not mine, be done." Does this seem twisted to you? Well, more's the pity. Because I say however you connect, whatever you connect with, the crucial thing is to connect.

When I first joined AA, I was one of those with that whole thing we refer to as "The God problem." "Pray? Really? You gotta be kidding!" It was so unnatural, so uncomfortable. "Do it anyway," my sponsor told me. Any lengths. It's always hardest the first time, and the second, and so on, until you know what? I kind of missed it when I didn't do it.

This was the amazing gift that Renascent gave me: a time to be quiet and still in a safe place, and to know that my higher power always was, and always is, with me. I had been raised to know God, and somewhere along the line I let go of that guiding hand.

I recall sharing my very personal take on my higher power with a (special) AA friend, and being told it was disrespectful and wrong to refer to almighty God as "baby." I had made that fateful mistake of falling into a relationship too early in my recovery and these words decimated me, eventually leading to a relapse. My sponsor had told me that we do not enter relationships in early recovery because we let that person become our higher power. I thought she was full of s@#*, until I came out the other end of my relapse. It's exactly what I did. I let someone else's judgment get in the way of my connection with my higher power.

When I started reading the Big Book, having my God hang-up, I substituted "universe" for "God." I've heard others say this, and I think I made a good beginning. Then came nature, then the fellowship of AA, and ultimately what a very wise woman called "Mother/Father God."

It doesn't matter what you call it. It matters that you know you are not it.

These are so many conceptions of higher power, and I incorporate as many of them as I encounter. One friend calls hers "Wolfie" after her animal totem. Another sees and hears a choir of angels, who want only for her to be healthy and well. And some go to church, and kneel. I'm not really a church-goer. But on those occasions when I do go, I feel moved by spirit.

My recovery has brought many gifts, and I think the most special is faith. Faith that life gets better when we take the right steps. Faith that in our darkest hours, we are truly not alone. Call it whatever you want, but do call it. It is what makes the whole journey possible.

And the best part of connecting with your higher power — gratitude. Thank you Mother/Father God, thank you Renascent and thank you AA. A life lived in gratitude is a life lived in light.

Keeping the Channel Open

Allan J. (Punanai 2005)

My first effective communication with my Higher Power was not in a place of worship or meditation. It happened while sitting in the back seat of a police car, staring at the grill ahead of me.

I had just had a "moment of clarity." Everything I had built up around myself — my wife and family, my work and reputation, my financial security — was about to come crashing down, I thought, as a result of my inability to control my drinking. I was either going to seek help or drink myself to death.

Out of nowhere I had the overwhelming feeling that everything was going to be alright. This strange, illogical feeling dissipated quickly as the police officer, returning from searching my vehicle, got in the front and started talking ... but it didn't leave me entirely.

Over the following days, I would return to examine that feeling, trying to rationalize it, but couldn't do so. Why, in the back of a police car in the depths of despair, should I start to feel optimistic about the future, I asked? One thing was clear to me, though: I was going to seek help rather than take the other route I had contemplated. That led me to Renascent.

In the weeks and months that followed, as I opened up in AA meetings, I came to meet others who, in different places but at the same point of desperation, had experienced the same feeling. Their knowing smiles as I shared and their comments afterward led me to believe that God had done for me something that I couldn't do myself — see hope at the point of absolute despair.

In my journey through the Steps of Alcoholics Anonymous, I have to find the way that works for me to keep the channel open with God. After all, he, she or it had been patiently waiting for me to stop shrieking selfish prayers along the lines of "get me out of this mess" for quite a while. Only in the back of the police car was I ready to communicate. It is up to me to create the state of mind where communication continues.

For a period, I thought I could combine it with religious interest in a church, and found that I couldn't. In particular, I can't relate to the stylized prose of most prayers. Each day now I start with the same simple request of God — to let me know my place, and accept it — for the day that is about to unfold. Throughout the day, I have to remind myself to "Let Go and Let God," as it is not in my nature to do so.

Sobriety has not changed my "control freak" tendencies, but staying in touch with my Higher Power makes it easier to change my behaviours. Now it is easier to know when to accept things around me and when it is up to me to do something (generally involving me, rather than others).

Some months after leaving Renascent, I was at a formal dinner in Dessau, Germany. The waiters were aggressively plying the wine and schnapps for toasts, and I had moved from saying "No, thank you" politely and turning my wine glass over to explaining quite sharply to the waiter to stop asking me — I had a medical condition and could not drink alcohol. I thought of leaving on the pretext of feeling ill, but that would have caused other complications. I sat back and "turned over" the issue.

In the midst of strangers across the table, a lady leaned forward, looked me straight in the eyes and said, "I understand. My husband is allergic to alcohol, too." And the pressure and anxiety lifted. I was not alone.

Quite frequently these days, I have similar "coincidences" resulting from this new course of action.

I am a scientist by profession. Yet, while I was drinking, I misread the second-most important experiment of my life — my ability to manage the consumption of alcohol. Time after time, I would replicate the same test under the same conditions and get the same result — me drunk or passed out. In the mindset of denial, my conclusion was, "Next time it will be different."

I have now had the benefit of many individual days in sobriety with this new, most important experiment of my life — that of asking for the right sort of help and turning over my will to God. It works for me. The results, whether the day brings good news or bad, are too consistent for me to misread, ignore or deny.

I hope that you too can find your own route to conversations with your Higher Power. It is worth the effort.

Invited to Spiritual Community

Leslie H. (Munro 2003)

The First Thing

"I used to have only two speeds," she said to us. "One-hundred-sixty-klicks-per-hour speed or dead-stop-paralysis speed."

It was the first time I heard this woman speak at a 12-step meeting, but it was as if she reached into my soul and found me. I identified.

I've been identifying with other recovered alcoholics and addicts for some time now. Identifying with their personal stories. Like my sponsor said to me the first time we sat in a restaurant where we met weekly to read the Big Book together, "the first thing is to identify."

> If you have a drinking problem, we hope you may pause in reading one of the forty-two personal stories and think: "Yes, that happened to me"; or more important, "Yes, I've felt like that"; or, most important, "Yes, I believe this program can work for me too."
> *Alcoholics Anonymous, p. xii*

"When I identify with the alcoholic/addict behaviour and identify with the feelings and thinking, then I have Step One. If I believe that this solution might work for me, too, and identify with that hope, then I have Step Two," she said.

The Two-Speed World

Until I was 17, the community I identified with was that "two-speed" world. A childhood home of parties or isolation, of crazed laughter or morning-after tears. Raging violence or vows it would never happen again. Dysfunctional attempts at communication or stonewalling silence. New promising places to live or shameful moving in the night. By the time I was 14, we had moved 14 times and I was effectively rootless, with no earthly idea of community or how to fit into one. I retreated into a fantasy world ... until one day that first drink and that first other drug came and invited me out.

I left home going 160 and basically didn't stop until I hit a wall. In between was a community that felt like it had been born for me. If community means "participation by all," then that was for me. I was the recruiter of anything that felt good and altered my state of being. You were either for me or against me. Even the sweet robins singing at dawn became enemies, because it meant the party was over. My community was a continual state of on or off, centred around how to get, use and then find a way to do it all again. The two speeds were my way or the highway.

> Until one day the switch seemed to be stuck on off. My community became a realm of one, behind closed doors, closed curtains, broken promises and broken relationships. My community had stopped taking my calls and I had become uninvited. I, who had wanted to be found so desperately, was now in permanent hiding.
> Further Along the Road Less Travelled
> M. Scott Peck

Dr. Scott Peck, an American psychiatrist and author, wrote that alcoholics are blessed. He believes that we are all "broken" — full of grief and terror — even if we are not fully aware of it. And we are doubly cursed because we don't talk to each other about these things, even though they are critical to our happiness. We hide behind masks of composure.

> Alcoholics [and addicts], on the other hand, are not any more broken than the rest of us but they are unable to hide it anymore. So the great blessing of alcoholism is the nature of the disease. It puts people into a visible crisis, and, as a result, into a community — an AA group.
> The Blessing of Alcoholism, Rupert Wolfe-Murray

My visible crisis was noticed by a recovered alcoholic because he identified with it. He asked, "Les, do you think you might have a problem with alcohol?" Although I didn't know it at the time, I had been invited to something that was to change my life profoundly. I had been invited to spiritual community.

How Strange ... and Even More Important

> *How strange that we should ordinarily feel compelled to hide our wounds when we are all wounded! Community requires the ability to expose our wounds and weakness to our fellow creatures. It also requires the ability to be affected by the wounds of others... But even more important is the love that arises among us when we share, both ways, our woundedness.*
> *The Different Drum: Community Making and Peace,*
> *M. Scott Peck*

True North

One of my dear friends today, a fellow traveller in recovery, centres her spirituality and practice in the native medicine wheel. We often share about how we are being re-aligned to our true north. Bill Wilson talks about this in his essay on faith in the little book The Best of Bill. He talks about the *compass* of "perhaps the most important expression to be found in our whole AA vocabulary: the phrase 'God as we understand him.'"

In sobriety, I have come to know there is so much more to life than two speeds. In fact, I believe there is not a "speed" as much as there is a circle of continual ebb and flow and vitality, like a wondrous, spinning wheel that ever points us to our true north.

Lately, I am experiencing challenges that are difficult to deal with ... left to my own devices. But that's the thing. I'm not left to my own devices. Today, I am part of a community — a community of "lifelong friends." (AA, p. 152)

That community reminds me (when I forget) that my "real reliance is always upon" the God of my Understanding and promises that my Higher Power "will show [me] how to create the fellowship [I] crave." (AA, p.164)

May we all experience this promise.

Befriending the God of My Own Understanding

Jamal M. (Punanai 2013)

As a Muslim man, my understanding was that I would be condemned to a very harsh punishment in the afterlife since I took part in certain activities that are forbidden in the religion of Islam. My drinking and use of other mind-altering substances alongside "getting with" the opposite sex outside of wedlock are not activities of the ideal Muslim man. I was well aware of this even before my very first drink or first sexual encounter.

Once I took that first drink, it was game on. I did anything to forget and hide the guilt, shame and fear that was engraved in my psyche. In my early reflections thus far (I will be one year sober on October 5, 2014), I think I was negotiating with God — as long as I did certain things that He liked, maybe I could still earn my ticket into Heaven.

Alcohol, of course, worked wonders for me in the early days of my drinking and I was able to justify my behaviour with minimal baggage. Since my intentions were generally good and I was only hurting myself by my drinking, my plan was to make up lost time with the guy upstairs in my later years.

My family migrated to Canada from Pakistan when I was 10 years old. I wanted to fit in so desperately that I developed what I have now come to believe was false pride. I think this idea of being superior was instilled in me by my family and the Muslim community at large. I didn't like this feeling at a younger age and I don't like it now at my current age of 35.

Please keep an open mind as this is only my personal opinion.

I thought that the conversations that took place during community events were fake and hypocritical. People spoke of wonderful ideals but there was no action. Inner peace and contentment were promised but were never evident.

I then decided to go my own way. I studied and worked hard and gained an in-depth knowledge of the Canadian financial landscape. I achieved financial success at relatively young age — the world was now open for business at Jamal's convenience.

I continued to gravitate further towards Western culture and very seldom sought help from my elders or God. I should also mention that most of the religious teachings and prayers in Islam are offered in the Arabic language — I do not speak or understand Arabic. I must also say that the fear-based approach in organized religion was not an attractive selling feature for me. The point I am trying to make is whether it was the language barrier, the lack of relatability, the constant fear-based teachings or the strict rules, I put in a good amount of effort to move away from religion.

Once alcohol stopped working, the fears and guilt crept up and I found myself at a very difficult crossroad. I could not pray for help because I did not have an understanding of or a relationship with God. I couldn't summon the courage to contact my religious community due to fears of being mocked and ridiculed.

But somewhere inside me I knew that God exists. This faint belief is something I am very grateful for. Once I was introduced to the Twelve Steps and gained a more thorough understanding of my forgiving God with infinite love and compassion, I took a hold of Him as the drowning seize life preservers.

I am grateful to my parents and to the religion of Islam for the knowledge that God exists. I am planning on learning more about the religion of Islam with a new pair of sober lenses and, of course, in English.

Religion taught me that my actions were sinful and that I would be punished in the afterlife. Twelve-step recovery taught me that I have a sickness and I can live a meaningful life in this lifetime. I am truly grateful to Alcoholics Anonymous for the strength to explore and befriend the God of my own understanding and for spiritual freedom.

Returning to My Spiritual Roots

Julie B.

I'm an urban Aboriginal person who was raised by a single mother of European descent.

Although I did beadwork and occasionally went to powwows, I didn't subscribe to — and was never really exposed to — any traditional Anishinaabe cultural practices or spiritual beliefs.

The only spiritual connection I had when I was drinking was that I worshipped my next bottle of wine. I drank heavily for over 20 years, and drank daily for the past 10. I was high-functioning for someone with extremely low expectations. For a long time, I knew that I was an alcoholic, but I didn't care.

Then one day I decided I wanted to live. When I finally sought treatment, I was drinking almost constantly from the time I woke up to the time I passed out at night. I had tried to stop repeatedly but I couldn't, and that scared the hell out of me.

When I first got sober, almost three years ago, I lost my connection to alcohol. Alcohol had been my constant companion and best friend, even though it was slowly killing me. I had abandoned my friends, family and myself in order to keep drinking. When I finally faced the world in sobriety, I felt empty and alone. As a result, I had to learn how to connect with people and myself all over again — or perhaps for the first time.

I first found a spiritual connection on a camping trip. I started taking photos of a chipmunk I'd befriended, and I was so lost in joy that I didn't feel the craving to drink.

I also went back to university. The first class I took was an introduction to Indigenous studies. While learning of the history of my ancestors, I often cried in class. But I also learned about the Indigenous beliefs of living in concert with nature, and how everything is interconnected. I learned about ceremony and resilience. I went to a powwow, where I just cried for all the trauma that my ancestors had endured. However, I also felt like I didn't belong. I didn't know anything about the dances, the regalia or the ceremonies, so I decided to learn more.

As I continued my formal education, I also started going to community events. I asked Elders for guidance on becoming more involved. Mostly, I just hung around, observed ceremonies and copied what other people were doing.

The first time I smudged, I felt a connection to something I can't fully understand. When I was surrounded by the smoke from the burning medicines, I felt a weight lift off my shoulders. It felt like going home to a place I'd never been before. I can't explain it — I just felt better.

I went to see a traditional counsellor for the first time right before a camping trip. After my counselling session, I had the most intensely spiritual moment of my life. Arriving at the campground as the sun was setting, I climbed a hill near the lake to make an offering and say a prayer. I had never prayed before, so I brought a photocopy of a prayer to the Great Spirit that I had grabbed from the lobby on my way out from meeting the counsellor. The prayer asked for strength and intelligence — not to conquer my enemies, but to fight the enemy within.

I left an offering of berries by a tree stump and walked down a granite slab to the water's edge. I was alone, overlooking a quiet beach. I closed my eyes for a few minutes to meditate.

When I opened them and looked across the water, a deer came out of the woods and stared right at me. I instantly felt a happiness that I had not felt in years. I was in awe, and crying tears of joy. Then another deer came out of the woods! I couldn't believe I was the only one there to see this. The deer were drinking from the lake, and one of them was playing with a frog. They were peaceful and carefree — two qualities that had been missing from my life since I quit drinking.

It's difficult to describe, but those few minutes felt magical and life-changing. I don't know if it was the result of the offering and prayer or just a coincidence, but I do know it was the most spiritual experience of my life. I also know that it never would have happened if I hadn't gotten sober. I had to become fully present in my life in order to experience that connection with nature.

This year, I plan to celebrate National Aboriginal Day with my friends, and if I cry at the powwow, they will be tears of gratitude for the gift of being alive.

Waiting for a Sign

Eddie G.

I was raised Roman Catholic. I come from a family who believe in going to church regularly and I honestly never really questioned the church, God or my family's beliefs. They did not push them on me.

In 1997, when I attended my very first Alcoholics Anonymous meeting, I was advised that I needed to have a Higher Power. Since I was in the local detox, there were copies of the Big Book available for the clients to read. In fact, the counsellors and other staff strongly suggested that the clients read this book.

The word "God" kept repeating itself in this heavily suggested book. The more I read, the more I felt like I had to become a Christian of some kind in order to belong to this organization called Alcoholics Anonymous. I certainly felt disconnected from both the members and the principles that they were preaching about.

It can be intimidating when you come into a meeting and hear all of these strangers talking about "God" and "Higher Power." It is especially frightening when you personally have absolutely no belief in such things and don't see the need to have to convert to some different type of religion in order to be able to get professional help while coming off alcohol and drugs (which is the reason that I went to the meetings in the first place). I didn't go to meetings to learn about religion; I went to arrest my illness of addiction!

The bottom line was that alcohol and drugs were my Higher Power. They were my comfort, my piece of mind, my pain reliever, my anxiety stabilizer and my courage to be the person that I wanted to be. The problem was that I was never able to become that person due to the substance abuse.

I became a self-absorbed, selfish, self-seeking guy who had no convictions in terms of my recovery. I did not want to let go. This led to years of being in and out of 12-step meetings, treatment centres, hospitals and other institutions.

My last binge was very painful and the repercussions gave me a willingness I had never had before. I had no idea what this Higher Power would look like or how I would be able to communicate with it. I just knew that I was going to have an open mind about this and do some positive things about my substance abuse in the meantime. I guess you could say that I was going to keep myself busy until I found my Higher Power!

I followed through with this part and waited patiently and openly for something or someone to give me some kind of sign. Nothing. No sign. No flash. I kept on doing the things that my sponsor recommended I do. I stopped drinking and using drugs. I started attending meetings on a regular basis and I started doing the Steps for the second time.

This time, I was doing the Twelve Steps with a different outlook and expectation. It was not a "show me the evidence and I will believe you" approach. Instead, I decided to take an honest look at myself and ask for help with the guidance of my sponsor and the advice of an addictions counsellor.

My perception of what a Higher Power is today is probably not what many other people would expect. It is not some image of Charlton Heston or the voice of Morgan Freeman guiding me through life. I believe that my Higher Power has given me the ability to identify my own weaknesses and to know my limitations. I guess I would say that my Higher Power is "Good Orderly Direction" and the group conscience of my family and the other members of my 12-step groups.

I spoke before about how I never had a "giant flash" or some obvious "spiritual awakening" but I can certainly see a huge difference in my quality of life. Since coming into recovery, I have graduated from college, was accepted into university, started working in a field that I love, and have had more stability than ever before. This has also given me a much deeper connection with my family, who I was basically estranged from for a number of years. They trust me today.

I still have bad days but I always look for something good that happened at the end of each one. I also have been given the gift of not craving drugs and alcohol anymore. I don't have to fight it; for whatever reason, that obsession has been lifted. How that happened I don't know, but I do know how relieved and grateful I am that it is gone!

Learning to Let My Light Shine

MJ (Munro 2011)

If I thought of the words creativity or art years back, it's likely that painting, acting, film, video, music, photography and dance would have been the main things that came to mind. However, I have since come to believe that so much of what is seen and heard on a daily basis is a form of creativity. It's incredible once you really start looking around.

From an early age, I can remember loving art and taking pride in the talents I had. Creativity is such a part of me that it has become abundantly clear that if I want to have a joyous and peaceful life, I need to stay connected to this energy and vibrancy that lives within me, which I believe is channelled to and through me by the Higher Power of my own understanding.

Or maybe I even have an Angel that is with me, just waiting for me to be cleared enough of all my stuff (which is why Program is such a vital part of all this), so that these works can be put into action. And an even crazier idea ... perhaps it is simply my very own spirit that is this creative force, as created by the most creative source of all.

Can you imagine? Let's just say there is a Higher Power who created all of us, and all of the ideas that have flowed out into this world, in all the countries, in all the stores, homes, theatres, bands, dances, songs, festivals, holidays ... how amazingly creative is this Higher Power!?! It blows my mind.

As much as angst, sadness, suffering and loss can spark some fascinating and moving paintings, music or choreography in my head, I would say that at this point of my journey, keeping my body, mind and spirit as healthy as I am able to, one day at a time, is probably the most important factor in me continuing on my creative path. It just so happens that when I am not "well," even though at times I can create something from it, it keeps me for the most part paralyzed and unable to do anything at all. Scarily enough, a year or five years of good intentions and project ideas can pass by just like that.

But one thing, if anything, that I would like to express is that I am right on schedule. I hope you don't mind me saying that I believe you are also right on schedule, whatever that may look or feel like to you at this time.

This is a very exciting topic for me. And at the same time, when I get excited and feel hope and positivity, and maybe even some self-esteem, I can get a bit caught in the following trap … it goes something like this: You know how earlier I said, "I can remember loving art and taking pride in the talents I had"? Well, me saying that at first felt good, and fun to share. But then seconds later my mind says, "People are going to think you are egotistical, you are bragging, that's not humble, that's prideful, grandiose." And this just leads to me feeling like I'm a horrible person and I shut down, do something self-abusive to shut off the good feelings, and then sit there paralyzed.

So, yes, I face some challenges while learning how to honour, explore and express the artist within. I am afraid to let my light shine. I am afraid my latest YouTube video will not go viral and that I really am an amateur going nowhere. I am also coming to realize that this is a way of life for me that brings a fantastic abundance of peace and joy, which is so fun to share with others.

I've been embracing baby steps. I have my keyboard and art supplies set up so that at any time I can access them with the least possible effort. I "trick" myself into painting, in the same way that I trick myself into doing more Step work in those times of procrastination: just one word on the paper is all you have to do tonight … just one dab of paint on the canvas … and before you know it, a couple of hours have peacefully and joyfully passed by.

My spirit is vibrant and awesome. It is filled with so much to express, I sometimes think that I have self-medicated in order to tame this lion within. It is my joy, challenge and responsibility to honour my life, my health and my recovery so that whatever is within me can be given away and shared. I am so grateful to all who have shared their light and joy in various forms with the world. Thank you.

Wishing you all the very best!

Finding a New Higher Power

Bob M. (Leslie 1987)

By the time I was 45 years old, I was in the advanced stages of alcoholism. I had attempted suicide and couldn't stop drinking.

I had gone to AA for several months and had stayed dry for about 10 months. I knew it was a good program for you guys, but I was different, so I stopped going to meetings.

Within six months, I was drinking around the clock and couldn't stop. At the hospital, I was introduced to Renascent. I went to the Leslie House — the best thing that could have happened to me.

I should say that I was active in church and knew "who and what" God was. I also knew He had no time for the likes of me, especially since I turned out to be an alcoholic.

It was at AA meetings that I found out about spirituality and also about a "Loving God." I was one of those who found my Higher Power, not in the sanctuary of the church, but in the basements at AA meetings, held in those churches.

I began going to AA retreats at Manresa in my fourth year of sobriety, and found them so helpful to my sobriety and sense of fellowship that I kept on going.

At my third retreat, however, I kept to myself a lot and was asked why I was isolating so much. I replied that some things in my life were getting better, but I still wasn't sure what AA, a Higher Power and not drinking were really accomplishing. Why was I still so dissatisfied with my sobriety and my life?

It was suggested that perhaps I should use this retreat to find out what was really at the core of my belief, my faith and my being. It was then that I spent some time outside the buildings of Manresa, in what is commonly called Mother Nature.

By the end of the retreat, I had found the answer I was looking for. It is described in excellent detail in the Twelve and Twelve, Step Seven:

I was afraid of not getting what I wanted and/or I was afraid of getting what I didn't want. This fear had wrapped its way around every facet of my life.

In the past, the magic of alcohol had always allowed me to get through every failure, success, loss, gain and feeling that I liked or didn't like. Now that the magic of King Alcohol had gone, what was I going to do for the rest of my life without my cure-all?

Working that Step Seven ("Humbly asked Him to remove our shortcomings") into my life was frustrating and difficult.

As Step Seven states in part:

> *The chief activator of our defects has been self-centered fear — primarily fear that we would lose something we already possessed or would fail to get something we demanded. Living upon a basis of unsatisfied demands, we were in a state of continual disturbance and frustration. Therefore, no peace was to be had unless we could find a means of reducing these demands.*

I saw that this fear governed my thinking. I then understood that *"my serenity is inversely proportionate to my expectations."*

That was the turning point for my belief in a Higher Power. I realized that I had to develop a thing called faith or belief in the God that was talked about so much in AA meetings.

A loving power, not a vindictive power; one that had time for the likes of me and one that would make me well again, providing I kept using the kit of spiritual tools provided in the Twelve Steps.

Almost 20 years later, I still find my Higher Power manifested in many different ways.

While on one of my nature walks at last year's Renascent Men's Retreat, I was thrilled to come upon a young white-tailed buck. I was able to photograph it, close up. It was like looking into the face of the God of my understanding.

God grant you all one more day of sobriety.

The Miracle of Meeting Ourselves

Leslie H. (Munro 2003)

*Every decision I make is a choice between a grievance
and a miracle. I let go of grievances and choose miracles.*
Deepak Chopra, The Heart Sutra Meditation

The book *Alcoholics Anonymous* encourages us to become "properly armed with facts" about ourselves so that we can help others. These are my facts as I know them now; what I was like and what I'm like today.

I lived in a hostile world. I walked in fear, doubt, negativity, suspicion and confusion. There were lots of storms, with little sun or joy. I hid to survive, I kept quiet, tried to stay invisible, while taking on responsibility for everything as my fault. I rarely smiled. I searched for rules so I could learn them and blend in. It was like following a map to another country, with the terrain constantly shifting and changing. I had no roots, no anchors. I was extremely shy and desperate for you to read my mind. Eventually I became an angry, rebellious teen, taking no responsibility for anything and rejecting all authority. I was now a walled-up runner.

And then alcohol and other drugs found me. I still remember the "click" and heat of my first drink and the mellow blanketing of my first use of other drugs. Suddenly, all was well with the world. I was to spend the next 37 years in an altered state, continuing my full flight from reality.

My healing, this "personality change sufficient to bring about recovery," has been both slow and gradual and turbulent and fast. I had a problem with alcohol but alcohol wasn't my problem … it's living happily and purposefully clean and sober that's the tricky part. Yet it's worth every effort, pain and tear, absolutely. The miracles of recovery are everywhere and ours for the taking. Here are just a few I've experienced.

With the gift of surrender, the compulsion to drink and use was lifted. I became willing to go to any length to get better. I asked someone to sponsor me. I did what I was told. I made meetings a priority. I started to study the textbook. My mind started opening. I began the lifelong practice of Step work. I cried. I laughed (clean, sober laughter ... there is nothing better). I began to thaw. I made service commitments. I started sponsoring others. I "fired" (in writing) my old concept of God; I chose a new one and began the most amazing relationship of my life with Him-Her, a partnership that gets stronger and better every day.

Today, I listen to the robin's song with sober joy at the beginning of my day, instead of altered dread at the end of a heavy night of using.

Today, my children want me in their lives. Today, I have a loving relationship with my family instead of cruel fighting and dysfunction. I have made both direct and living amends.

Today, I get to choose to greet the woman in the glass with the eyes and thoughts of love. Instead of self-loathing, I increasingly have true compassion for myself and thus can extend that to others. More and more, I ask what's in it from me, instead of for me.

Today, I am teachable instead of ornery. Today, I can speak up for myself, calmly and surely. Today, I understand the difference between isolation and solitude. Today, I can ask for help to meet the ups and downs of life with serenity and grace. Today, I can look after fixing leaks in the roof without ripping up the basement. Today, I can list my good qualities as well as my shortcomings. Today, I smile and mean it.

My sponsor always says, "Sobriety rocks!" I remember wanting to believe that so badly. Today, I know it's true. Do that. Believe that. Stay a little longer. Try a little harder. We are all miracles, and what a miracle to meet ourselves, our true, transformed selves on the path. It is an experience you don't want to miss. May our clean and sober dates never change.

God, The Ultimate Scientist

Trevor B. (Punanai 2007)

> *Biophilia: The love of life or living systems; the connections that human beings subconsciously seek with the rest of life. The possibility that the deep affiliations humans have with nature are rooted in our biology.*

I used to think of myself as a scientist, believing in nothing of God or a spiritual plane of existence, or a spiritual way of life for that matter, but only in a chance meeting of the proper chemicals and conditions that gave birth to protozoan life that evolved into the living planet we inhabit today.

Some of the most brilliant scientific minds in history (even though starting their careers with faith only in the quantitative and measurable, and having a non-existent faith in an all-creating Higher Power) have developed a solid belief in the unseen and intangible as they break down the very fabric of space and time and the building blocks of matter that compose our known universe.

The scientist responsible for mapping the human genome declared, "We must have been designed by a higher intelligence," upon realizing the sheer genius, balance and numbers involved in chromosomal development. Mind-numbing!

A quote of Albert Einstein, one of the most revered scientific minds in history, that I find most fascinating is, *"God doesn't play with dice with the world."* I interpret this to mean that even in chaos there is balance. Nothing happens by chance. Everything happens for a reason.

Now when I walk through the woods I think of all that's going on around me; the balance of eco-systems, the weak, sick and old becoming prey for the strong and fit to complete the cycle of life.

I see blossoming flowers ripe for a bee to collect its nectar, then the bee buzzing about pollinating other flowers. I watch the order found in a colony of ants industriously fortifying their hill. I think of the chemical reactions taking place for a leaf to convert sunlight energy into food for itself, while metabolizing the carbon dioxide that we exhale into oxygen that it breathes out for us to inhale.

The balance and pattern of the way our physical world is governed is truly mind-boggling.

When it comes to biophilia, my testament is that I always, always feel recharged, calmer, replenished and grounded from having a closer contact with my Higher Power after being in close proximity to all Its miraculous creations.

I've discovered quite a number of new "thinking spots" in the downtown Toronto area. I highly recommend (just to name a few):

- Evergreen Brickworks on the Bayview extension; a great place to take in nature's beauty, with the city skyline as your backdrop to walk with your thoughts in quiet prayer and meditation
- High Park, especially during the cherry blossom season — stunning
- Trinity Bellwoods Park, for throwing the ball or disc around while catching some rays
- Allan Gardens with its greenhouse collection of flora and fauna

God is the ultimate scientist. The balance of the natural world is astounding, and it's simple, beautiful, glorious.

A Glimmer of Hope

Anne M. (Munro 2009)

Today I am sitting on a bench in the Toronto Necropolis. It is springtime and I am sober and it is a beautiful day.

I come here to visit my darling cousin Paul, whose name is on a plaque where his ashes were scattered. Paul was taken by AIDS 10 years ago.

I recall my last private visit with Paul two days before he died. I parked at St. Mike's Hospital armed with an unbearable sadness and a water bottle full of vodka. My bottle never contained water, and this day was no different. But Paul was dying and I had come to say goodbye.

After many swigs of vodka, I located and entered Paul's room. He had gone downhill so quickly this time, and he would not recover. Another swig. I sat down.

Paul was conscious but very weak. We shared a sweet kiss and a tender hug. How frail he was! I read to him an email from my mom, his beloved Aunt Mary. The two had always been so close, and it was heartbreaking to read her touching goodbye to him.

Paul managed a wee smile and then closed his eyes. I quietly watched him for awhile, and then suddenly his eyes opened. Wide. He raised his upper body from the bed, all the while looking intently at a point on the ceiling. He sat there, upright and transfixed, for what seemed like forever. His eyes never blinked, and he looked to be in awe.

Finally, he sank back into his pillow and looked directly at me. He then gently said, "Annie, my darling cousin. You must know that alcohol will kill you. It may take you slowly, like AIDS has taken me, but it will kill you just the same."

Wow. We didn't really say much more that day. I found it odd that he would say this and choose this time to say it. How strange this seemed to me. As far as I knew, Paul didn't know I had a "drinking problem." We had talked about everything under the sun over the years, but never this.

I put my memories of that day aside for another eight drunken years, until I crash-landed at my inevitable bottom. Three years ago I was beaten by the man I loved in a drunken rage. He was arrested and I found myself jobless, homeless, and with no belongings save for some clothes and a suitcase. I drank and I drank, but it was never enough. The pain was unbearable. The anger was intense.

I dragged myself from place to place, crashing with whoever would have me. It became impossible to find comfort even with my family. I was sick and in pain and pushing away those who loved me most. I ended up at Filmores Hotel here in Toronto. Yes, that Filmores.

After just one devastating, gut-wrenching week there, I picked up the phone and called Alcoholics Anonymous. I had called many times in the past, but this time I connected with a kind and compassionate woman. She told me of a women's meeting at 11:00 the next morning. The LCBO didn't open until noon. I dragged my shaking, sick and exhausted carcass to that meeting. It was in that blessed hour that something changed in me. For the first time in forever I found a glimmer of hope, and I hung on to that with everything I had. It wasn't much, but it was a start. My first true awakening came on February 8, 2009.

That I was powerless over alcohol was obvious to me. It was a fact I accepted deep within myself from the very start. Steps Two and Three, however, presented an enormous barrier to my continuing in AA and staying sober. I found it necessary to unburden myself of any vestiges of my childhood faith, as I felt only deep resentment when I went there. I became willing to do whatever was necessary, because I knew my life depended on it.

So I surrendered. I dumped all the crap, everything I knew or thought I knew, and began from ground zero. I watched you, I listened to what you had to say, and I followed in your footsteps. I became willing. I became teachable. And, yes, it was not easy.

I "came to believe that a Power greater than ourselves could restore us to sanity," as our Step Two says, excruciatingly slowly. At first, I clung to the rooms of AA and my beloved Big Book and all of my fellow travellers on the road to recovery. I entered Renascent in March 2009 and it was there I found true acceptance and guidance and hope. And the comfort of being surrounded by other women in recovery. I was no longer alone.

I left Renascent to live at Street Haven, a women's shelter. It was there, late at night in a noisy room with five other women, that I took my Step Three. I began to see that my Higher Power had a plan for me and I felt deeply cared for and loved. The lovely home in Bloor West Village where I was assaulted was worlds away, and I was perfectly okay with it all. I began to learn humility at Street Haven, and it felt good.

Today, over two years and four months sober, I reflect with gratitude on my journey in recovery. I am deeply grateful for all the pain, because it prepared me for the awakening. I meditate and pray like I breathe; they fit so naturally into my life today. I continue to attend and love AA meetings, am involved in service, and meet regularly with my amazing sponsor. I do my best to carry the message and stay connected. I value my sobriety above all else, because without it, I would be nothing. And for that, I am truly grateful.

And today I know, wherever my darling cousin Paul may be, he is smiling.

How Recovery Changed My Christian Experience

George Z.

When I was asked to write this article, I immediately said yes, but then wondered if I'd been too hasty in my reply. The first questions that popped into my mind were, "Am I really a Christian?" and then "How would I define what that means for me?" So this is where I must start.

To be a Christian, for me, simply means that I *try* to follow the teachings of Jesus of Nazareth as laid out in the main text of the New Testament. I see his teaching and my experience of that teaching in the same way my Buddhist friends describe their experience of taking refuge in the Buddha, the Dharma and the Sangha.

So as a Christian, I would say Jesus is the teacher, the gospels are the teaching, and the community is the believers who try to practice the gospel of Love, Forgiveness and Service, while bringing others who wish to to the same experience.

My religious experience growing up was Roman Catholic, with a French-Canadian mother and an Italian immigrant father. The church was very important to them and it became important for me too. I was an altar boy (who helped himself to the wine), I went to Catholic school, and I had the requisite guilt about all things sexual — and learned what could cause blindness in a "good Catholic boy."

I remember the fire and brimstone sermons by Father Hogan. I was shaking in my boots ... but, alas, teenage years and a public high school, booze, drugs, parties ... the guilt was still there, but now I'd decided that if I couldn't be good, I'd be good at being bad!

Thus was my confused sense of faith as I discovered recovery in my early 20s. So I took the Big Book seriously and tried to rediscover the religion of my youth. There, I found some amazing people who taught me about life — a life motivated by love and healing.

I discovered how to have a real relationship in marriage, and the humility and "all in" approach of St. Francis, St. Benedict and the Monastic Experience. In reading John Main, I learned how to meditate, the true meaning of the Christian sacraments, and a real sense that I could never be far from a loving creator, only I was closed off to the reality of that presence in my life. St. Francis modelled a literal poverty; Jesus spoke of poverty of spirit in the Sermon on the Mount (translated humility); St. Benedict showed me that discipline is freedom.

As I continued to pray and meditate and went more deeply into the Steps of recovery, I discovered a universal language that had its roots in Christianity but was able to translate and communicate the central message of love, forgiveness, healing and service in a way that was open to all beliefs ... a miracle if there ever was one.

So how would I describe my Christian experience in recovery? How well do I follow the principles of my faith?

Well, I guess I'd have to say I am able to be a good Christian "now and then" and although I practice that faith in a Roman Catholic Christian church, recovery has taught me not to confuse the flavour with the ice cream ... the teachings of Jesus are the ice cream ... the church the flavour.

And I do like my ice cream!

My Higher Power — Spirit Wolf

Robyn H. (Munro 2011)

Years before I came into the program of AA, I was already being guided by my Higher Power — only I wasn't aware of it at the time.

I spent a good portion of my life searching for something that would fill the large void that I felt inside of me. I sought to find my god and strength in the church and in mainstream religion, but nothing seemed to fill the emptiness in my life. For me, alcohol was the answer for a very long time. I drank to forget friends I couldn't make and I drank to find friends, to feel wanted and loved.

Drinking took me only to very deep, dark, dismal places where I was totally blinded and could not see the world around me. All I could see was a brick wall all around me with no way out. Little did I know that my Higher Power was with me guiding me down those dark paths and catacombs and teaching me lessons along the way that would give me the strength and courage and insight that I have today.

Ever since I was a child, I had always loved the song of the wolf. I remember hearing the wolves across the lake in the early evening at the cottage. I would sit on the beach and listen and call out to them, hoping for an answer back, never knowing that these experiences would shape my life in the future.

As I grew up, I forgot those special moments I had on that beach. Lost in the ravages of alcoholism, I forgot the power and symbolism of what the wolf meant to me.

I came back into the rooms of AA in 2011. My visit, yet again, to Women's Own Detox was definitely planned by my Higher Power. While I was there, a sponsor asked me if I prayed. I didn't, but since I was there once again with nothing to lose because I had lost it all, I decided to give it a try.

For the first time ever I got down on my knees and prayed: "I don't know who or what I am praying to, but I want to live, and I need help." That night before I went to sleep, I looked out the window of Women's Own and noticed that the billboard outside the window was advertising whiskey. "How ironic," I thought. But when I awoke the next morning, that billboard had been changed overnight. It was now an advertisement for Great Wolf Lodge. I still get chills every time I think about this.

When I look back over my drinking career, I see several times where the wolf was present in symbolism or thought. I even once got a wolf tattooed on my leg, "just because."

I truly believe that my Higher Power, which I call my "Spirit Wolf," found me and guided and held me through many dark times when I couldn't do it myself. The god of my understanding represents strength, love, courage, friendship, family and freedom.

These are qualities which today, with the help of my Spirit Wolf, I am learning about, one day at a time.

Connecting to the Source

John G. (Punanai 2005)

My first sincere prayer as a grown man went something like this, "If there's anything out there, please help me."

Although I had little hope that my plea would be heard and even less hope that it would be answered, I did know one thing for sure. I was killing myself with drugs and alcohol and I could not stop. I wasn't looking to become enlightened, for eternal life, or even to become a better person. I just needed something that could save me from myself.

Suddenly, I was given the clarity to see through my denial. I saw my life for what it had become: a colossal mess. I knew I needed to do something drastically different and I received the courage to seek help.

I was taught that by asking for power, I could stay clean one day at a time. I found this to be true and miraculously the days turned into weeks and the weeks turned into months.

This simple cry for help was the beginning of a wonderful relationship. Every day that I didn't have to poison myself was further evidence that some force was working in my life. I was given a daily gift of freedom from self-destruction. I realized that my very existence depended upon my connection to this power. Miraculously, the obsession to use had been removed and I was now able to begin to learn how to live.

The God of my understanding is still, to some extent, beyond my understanding. I have found that what I believe in is not as important as the fact that I believe in something. I have tapped into an incredible source of power that fills that black hole inside me and enables me to deal with life.

My morning routine, though somewhat awkward at first, has become as natural as getting dressed. A daily reading from a 12-step-based publication helps me to get focussed. I must acknowledge the fact that I have a sickness that needs treatment. I then quiet my mind through a short, simple meditation, which helps to clear the connection with my higher power. I then talk to my God as if we were face to face.

My prayer process has changed quite a bit over time. What started as simply, "Please keep me sober today" in the morning and "Thank you" at night has gradually transformed into a beautiful exchange of words, ideas and emotions.

At first, my defiance prevented me from getting on my knees to pray. I felt that it wasn't necessary. I still feel that God hears me no matter what position I'm in, but out of a sincere sense of great gratitude and a realization that everything valuable in my life is a gift from God, I pray on my knees whenever possible.

It is easy to get caught up in everyday life and drift away from the spirit. It is usually when I am in this distanced state that old thinking will start to creep in. I may become less tolerant and more judging of others and society in general. My focus often shifts from my many gifts to every little thing that isn't exactly the way I think it should be in my life. Consequently, I can go from gratitude to self-pity in no time at all. Lack of motivation and indecision are two other common warning signs. Fortunately, these are usually short-term states. I find that specific and persistent prayer always leads me back to a sense of peace.

Very early in recovery I did service work for one reason only: because I was told it would help keep me sober. And it did. Today, I consider it a privilege and a pleasure to carry the message of hope. I find it very rewarding to be of help to anyone, in or out of recovery, rather than the force of destruction that I used to be.

Turning it over has been a difficult concept for me to grasp. It is totally contradictory to my old way of life. I used to bombard situations with my ideas and willpower in an effort to get them to go my way. More often than not, the results were disappointing. The more I tried to force things, the worse the outcome.

By letting go, I gain a great sense of relief that the problem is in much more capable hands than mine, and the confidence that the outcome — even if I don't like it — will ultimately be in my best interest. By doing what I believe is right instead of being controlled by selfish motives, I can live with a clear conscience and a firm belief that everything in my life is just the way it ought to be.

Just as my sobriety depends heavily on my awareness and connection to my higher power, my peace and serenity depend on the growth and development of my personal relationship with my God.

Fine-tuning My Spiritual Ears

Carolyn K.

Many years ago, my family and I experienced the devastating powerlessness of watching one of my beloved brothers die in a very slow and excruciating way. Before this, I had not known that human suffering could descend into such an abyss.

At that time, I was a mere 22, and it was during this period that I almost completely lost my faith in God, in hope, in just about anything at all. Fear took hold of me. I was almost completely self-propelled by my own will; barely moving through the surface of life, secretly holding on by my fingertips and making choices that seemed to be appropriate at that time.

I met and married a wonderful, loving man, had two beautiful children, and developed a successful career. But none of this could keep the gnawing sense of growing fear at bay: the futility and meaninglessness that my brother's death had left me with.

This fear just kept growing within me, like a virus, rippling through me right beneath the surface, but staying deep enough that no one was aware of it but me. Of course at the time I kept it all inside, hoping that the awful memories would just someday disappear. What I didn't realize was that while I could hope all I wanted, the thing that was slowly disappearing was me!

Silence and stillness threatened and terrified me, since that is the place that I intuitively knew something mysterious was present, and it was a relationship that I didn't want to have. God had betrayed and violated my trust, and I would never have anything to do with that again. I closed off my ears to the voice of Spirit, and could hear only the terrifying roar of the fear that fed my Ego.

Alcohol, being the "voracious creditor" that it is, took me down fast and furiously. In a period of eight months, I went from being a normal social drinker to nearly dead — a blessing in the sense that unlike so many others, I didn't have to suffer the prolonged years of the development of the disease and the personal losses that come with it.

Thanks to a very powerful Spiritual Experience that jolted me out of this Ego state, my life was spared from destruction. A new relationship was born: one with a God of my own experience and understanding.

I have to become quiet to connect with that relationship, but when I do, it is always there, gently, lovingly whispering to me at the core of my being. If I can't connect to it, it is not because it's not there, but because I have too much going on in my life to enable me to hear, much like trying to tune in to a radio frequency that is experiencing a lot of static disruption!

Today, whenever I begin to feel what Carl Jung refers to as "existential angst," chances are that I'm slipping on my Eleventh Step meditation practice. There are no reasons for this, only excuses. If I listen carefully, I can hear the soft, quiet inner voice of wherever I am — jogging, teaching yoga, listening to clients or doing the dishes.

To listen carefully, I have learned to stop what I am "do-ing," become completely still, and enter into the silence of "be-ing" (even though I now have three boisterous boys, I have discovered the wonders of earplugs — you know those neon orange bell-shaped ones?). This voice of my HP is my conscious contact, and the source of my serenity today.

It has become more real to me than anything extraneous, and it is the most beautiful, intimate and important relationship I have in my life today. Everything else flows from that inner spring: my continued recovery, my marriage, children, career and teaching.

With my daily meditation practice, I have become deeply centred in a moment-to-moment awareness of the presence of my HP that never shifts or changes. It is an unconditional and abiding presence that shines from the inside out and never abandons or betrays. It never hurts. It never confuses or abuses.

It is the place where I have found peace in my heart, and it is the place where I can come to surrender my weariness, frustrations and heartbreaks at the end of each day. It keeps me moving forward, and quenches my spiritual yearning and thirst for healing and wholeness. Although sometimes the world can seem harsh, it is the inner sanctuary where my peace and serenity flourish. I am forever grateful.

As the yogis say, Namaste.

Drawn to Darkness, Pushed Back to Light

Rahim J. (Punanai 2011)

The concept of spirituality that I understood as I was raised stemmed from the teachings and practices of my religion, Islam.

Meditation and service were essential factors of my faith but as I grew older, I was drawn more towards service because of the friendship, escape and fun that I lacked when I was at home. Meditation was never "pushed" on me by my parents, although they kept talking about how important it was in our faith.

Another concept I learned through my faith was having balance between the spiritual and material life — to have one without the other, or to have too much of either, wasn't considered good.

As I grew older, I was more attracted to the fun and escape I found in material life. There was a deficit I had always felt growing up and I was able to fill it up with social bonds and adventures. As time went on, practice in my faith diminished and I relished the occasional escape and fun I had with friends, which led to the beginning of my using and drinking just before I turned 13.

Almost three decades went by and my search for escape and fun, fuelled by alcohol and sometimes other substances, led me down a dark tunnel. In all this time, I was able to get an education, an awesome career, and a wife and son too. I spent years managing the balance between my material life and my addiction. The light of spirituality was but a memory, although I did pray desperately when I found myself in feelings of remorse, guilt and fear.

When the rooms of AA found me, I was told that a God of my understanding would restore my sanity. I couldn't remember any time in my life that I had lived in sanity. What I had portrayed on the outside was never in synch with what was going on inside my head. Dishonesty and manipulation had become second nature, almost like survival skills. In the last years of my drinking, I didn't understand why I couldn't stop, even knowing what the consequences would be.

As my sponsors guided me through the Twelve Steps, and as I got active in service, it was suggested to me to begin praying and meditating. It wasn't until I had completed my Fourth and Fifth Steps that I was able to stop thinking for a measurable amount of time.

The unconditional love and support I found in the fellowship started filling that age-old, dark deficit I always had, through the light of service and unity. It wasn't until I got to know myself better, cleaned my side of the street, and loved others unconditionally that I was able to understand what spirituality meant to me.

I had a spiritual awakening as a result of these Steps and I have started on a journey in search of the God of my understanding.

Spiritual Awakenings, Renewed Perceptions

Marnie S.

Throughout my 20s and 30s I felt that I needed something "deeper" in my life. I couldn't define what that was, yet there seemed to be something missing from my core. Growing up with an alcoholic parent and living with addicted partners added to the "God-sized" hole in my spirit. My low self-esteem and recurring sense of insecurity and abandonment were draining me. What could help alleviate this emptiness?

In my 40s, I was about to move to a new city to be with a man I had reconnected with after many years. He was one year sober and attended AA diligently. I figured I had finally hit the jackpot. An amazing person and he didn't drink?! Being with a sober person was foreign to me. All my previous experiences in relationships had been with drinkers. I was up for the challenge — after all, I thought, doesn't love conquer all?

I didn't know anything about AA, but I had heard of Al-Anon years before when my sister had told me that she attended meetings and that our father was an alcoholic — a statement that I laughed at, but silently questioned. So I figured that I would attend a few Al-Anon meetings with the hope of being fully prepared for my new relationship. My two intentions were to find out what AA was all about and to get instructions on how to keep my partner from drinking.

At the first meeting I attended, I heard a lot about God. I was skeptical. I heard people laugh and I heard people cry. I sat very silently with my pen and paper, ready for the answers I was hoping to hear. Those specific answers didn't come, but the shares I heard were like nothing I had heard before. Stories of struggles, triumphs and self-discovery. There was vulnerability without judgment happening all around me. I could barely say my name for fear of saying something silly. When the meeting finished, I darted quickly out of the room. I figured I wouldn't be there long; no need to get to know anyone.

I moved to the new city a few days later and began attending more meetings, mainly because my partner was often out at AA meetings. It also gave me an excuse to figure out my way around the new city. I still sat silently in those meetings, not knowing how to articulate my thoughts and feelings, still waiting to hear how to keep him sober.

Slowly, something started to happen. I began to leave those meetings feeling pretty good. I began thinking less about my partner and his plight and more about me and my actions/reactions. I started to have the occasional "spring in my step" and I would even feel moments that I can only describe as "joy." My soul felt as though it was beginning to defrost.

I read the literature, took service positions and attended meetings regularly. I was feeling a greater sense of connection with members and the literature, but after a few years, the little faith I had gained began to falter. I wasn't moving any deeper into recovery. I was stuck. I started building up walls again, went to meetings less often and began to feel alone, distrustful and blaming. I had meeting recovery, but no spiritual connection. I became so hopeless about life that I considered not wanting to be in this world.

There I was, learning a new way of living through a 12-step program and I was hitting my own bottom? How could it be? The truth slowly became clear: I hadn't worked the whole program, just bits and pieces of it. I hadn't been willing to get a sponsor and work the Twelve Steps, two of the most important tools of the program! I hadn't been willing to ask for help.

After weeks of pain, I mustered the courage to ask a member to be my sponsor. Slowly, I began to work the Steps with her. I still couldn't fully grasp the parts about God but I kept trying (often with resistance and skepticism). Eventually, I got some momentum and moved through the Steps.

Sharing one-on-one with someone through the Steps brought me the priceless gift of trust. Beginning to trust someone with all my secrets and character defects allowed me to start to see that if I could have trust in her, I could have trust in a power greater than me. It was clear that she trusted a greater power, people in the rooms of AA did, why couldn't I?

Having trust in a sponsor has helped me to shelve my will and let God and others in. The more I began practicing new behaviours and letting go of my need to control outcomes (and what my partner may or may not do), the more I would get these small zaps of awakening delivered in the forms of less worrying, more compassion and more self-esteem. I began to feel a deeper connection to a power in my life. It was sort of like the wind — I could feel it but I couldn't see it.

Connecting and sharing what is truly going on inside with someone one-on-one has taught me about relationships and what healthy ones are. I believe that my universal spirit delivers messages through others, and being willing to listen has granted me fresh outlooks. These changes in perception are my spiritual awakenings.

I still haven't heard the answer to my initial inquiry of "how to keep my partner from drinking." But I no longer seek the answer to this. It's funny how the reason I sought help in recovery was because of my partner's sobriety and now the truth of why I stay is for my own emotional sobriety.

Today, I am more aware of the tools available for me to connect with my Higher Power, to be able to have those "aha" moments. I have choices such as getting to a meeting, praying, sharing with others or calling my sponsor. As long as I practice staying open during a crisis, I know that I am headed out of the valley and towards the peaks in life.

Allowing Love to Enter

Jason A. (Sullivan 2006)

When everything else is gone, all that remains is God.

In the end, I was a slave to my craving to drink. I had lost all choice in the matter. I had to drink or I would surely die. No part of my day had any higher purpose than the acquisition and consumption of alcohol. Now that I am recovered, how do I train myself to fight the resentments that will surely keep me just as enslaved as the drink — a prisoner in my own mind?

As a younger man, the accumulation of material wealth was a major driving force in my life. If only I had an unlimited supply of cash for my booze, and a house and car to impress the in-laws and the neighbours, everything would be alright. So what is my goal, my purpose in life, now that the material things that used to define me no longer hold any meaning?

As I grow in sobriety, I realize that the only wisdom I can learn is the wisdom of humility. To be able to say, "I don't know" and ask a power greater than myself for help. In my experience, the mantra of a spiritual warrior is "Success Through Surrender."

When we stop fighting everything, because we have to, we find an inner peace that as active alcoholics and addicts we could never experience. The last thing I ever thought of doing as a practicing alcoholic was letting God handle my affairs, and I certainly wasn't in any shape on Sunday mornings to attend a church! But I have found that there are as many variations on the spiritual experience, and as many forms of God, as there are people in the world.

A power greater than ourselves certainly does not have to be the God of any organized religion. But it can be. I do know that whatever conception I happen to formulate about a Higher Power is still not complete. We're limited to human experience, human perception and human language to try to explain something much vaster than can even be imagined.

So how do I, an insane, shattered man, hope to attain any kind of connection, a conscious contact, with God? The Twelve Steps are a good way to start.

In the early days, when the obsession to drink was lifted, I was elated, on top of the world. Experiencing the world through clear eyes, seeing and feeling the love of my children, gaining friends and fellowship all around — what an exhilarating feeling!

But behind those clear eyes, an alcoholic mind still lurked. Complacency and procrastination rapidly brought forth more insanity than I ever felt when drinking. Without the alcohol to dull the tongue and slow the mind, my insensitive words and actions came out in full force, and a true love I would gladly give up my life for slipped away.

Life still goes on and every day cannot be a bowl of cherries. When I get up in the morning and ask God for another day of sobriety, sometimes that's *all* I get. And in the past, there couldn't be a better reason to drink. But because of the Steps, I am able to reach out to God in new and deeper ways when everything else is in chaos.

An added benefit is that by working the Steps continually, and becoming a better person because of that work, I can learn to avoid chaos before it happens. Every step taken with purpose on the pathway of life uncovers another level of awareness and understanding of my Higher Power and his will for me.

The Prayer of St. Francis, commonly called the Eleventh Step prayer in recovery, is a powerful tool for getting out of myself, giving more of me, and accepting people, places, and things for what they are — other creations of God, just like me.

God is in the details. Taking the time to notice a flower in bloom, a child at play, waves rolling onto the beach or an act of kindness towards another person reminds me that the beauty of God is all around me.

There are many words of wisdom written that reflect similar spiritual journeys to the one I'm taking in recovery, and I find comfort in seeing that others have travelled this way before me. *The Art of*

Peace (or Aikido) is a Japanese writing that I've often found reflects the way I think of my ongoing spiritual awakening. *The Art of Peace* has no form — it is the study of the spirit. Likewise, everyone's personal spiritual journey in recovery is different.

The way of the spiritual warrior is not always easy. Fighting through personal demons and wreckage from the past to allow love to enter my heart was the first challenge. There continue to be internal struggles to justify my actions or shirk any responsibility for the chaos around me. Then there is the cutting away at defects of character that block my Higher Power and my ability to love myself and others.

The reward is the ability to behave according to God's will for me, with honesty and integrity. Even when the path seems impossible, it's the anticipation of learning what God's plans are for me, and developing a deeper understanding of myself and the world around me, that keep me moving forward.

A Skeptic's Journey to a Higher Power

Lisa N.

The struggle I've had finding a real Higher Power has been 17 years long, and it turns out that that Higher Power was so simple I almost missed it. If you are like me, perhaps my experience will be useful somehow. Here is what happened.

Round 1 — I Came:

I walked into AA 18 or 19 years ago. The God Issue turned me off completely as I was an atheist; the notion of a Higher Power was not only foreign to me but seemed a bit ridiculous. I stayed for about nine months, found a Higher Power in the form of a tall, dark, and handsome addict who had been in AA for 15 years yet was unable to stay sober. Suffice it to say things did not go well.

Round 2 — I Came To:

I returned to AA. I was properly defeated, beaten, bruised and willing to entertain the notion that there might be a power that could help me stay sober. They said, "Fake it till you make it" and that the group could be my Higher Power.

Thankfully, I saw many alcoholics in the rooms of AA staying sober under conditions much worse than my own. This inspired me, and the collective wisdom of the group coupled with the literature became my Higher Power.

I got a sponsor, got rid of the addict and started working the Steps. I got very active in AA and in my new life. Thanks to the program, I haven't had a drink since February of 1998. I haven't been perfect and have had many struggles since. "Progress, not perfection" are words I truly live by today — and without alcohol, I can manage to progress.

My sponsor told me to adopt the attitude, "Take what you like and leave the rest for now." Often the things I left would make sense later on. The important thing was to focus on what I related to rather than the things to which I did not.

So, "turning it over" in Step Three simply meant moving on to the next Steps. Six and Seven were a little tricky but I managed to interpret them without the need of "God the Father." For Step Eleven, prayer became my ongoing dialogue with the "universe," akin to doing affirmations. I practiced moving meditation through yoga and exercise. I found an amazing church that spoke about joy and love — a language I could hear.

Fast forward eight years. I was still not a believer in a supernatural being who has a hand in the day-to-day affairs of humans. For me, that never felt like truth. Although it is said in AA literature that your Higher Power can be a God of your understanding, I felt uneasy about mine being so different. The God most addicts shared about in meetings (and in the literature) was out there somewhere, personified as a "Him," and had its hand in the material world in a rather arbitrary way. I could not relate at all.

Around 10 years of sobriety, I felt like I was a fraud. I just didn't have a God. The Group of Drunks (GOD) was no longer enough to keep me sober because I began to see great (human) fallibility. So I decided not to go to meetings any more, as they no longer were a source of inspiration. This did not go particularly well. And that was the end of Round 2.

Round 3 — I Came to Believe:

Oddly, I am still atheist/agnostic, a skeptic and a science lover. However, there was something I had missed, and I had to fall and struggle to find it. That struggle brought me into another 12-step fellowship, as it was apparent that I was again powerless and needed to be restored to sanity. Frankly, it was a miracle I didn't drink.

This time, however, I don't feel pressured to believe what others believe any more. I have completely let go of what others think of me and my Higher Power. As a result, I have come to a Higher Power that is deep within and a very real part of me. I have often heard people say, "You need a God, just make sure it isn't you." But I personally needed a Higher Power that was part of me.

Turns out I had one! Here's what it is ...

I have always had a sharply intuitive voice of truth deep within me. I feel it in my stomach. When I listen to it, synchronicity always happens, life flows like a gentle river and my heart feels lighter. When I don't listen, chaos inevitably ensues. It is ever-present. I never ever considered that this was actually my Higher Power — it was too simple!

I'm not sure where intuition comes from, whether it's a biological imperative genetically coded into our cells for survival, or if it has a connection to something bigger. I do know that I can "plug in" or "unplug" from the power. When I plug in, I am in that flow. Life is simple, without struggle, chaos or drama. When I unplug, life is an uphill battle that is meaningless, and I am left in the deep, dark, black hole I call "The Void."

How do I plug in?

- Being an active part of a like-minded group like a 12-step program. Going to meetings and being around people who are striving to walk a spirit-centred life as opposed to an ego-centred life.

- Fitness: It has saved my life. I suffer from clinical depression, and being active keeps my endorphins high and staves away the darkness.

- Connection with others: Keeping in contact with a small but healthy circle of friends is key. It has been proven that just being with another person raises our serotonin levels — which tells us we are programmed to be in a community.

- Conversely, removing myself from toxic and addicted people is imperative.

- I love to read or listen to podcasts about science, psychology and spirituality. These tools help me see the universe and our place in it as a wonderful, majestic mystery.

Thanks to my sponsor, a new outlook and recovery program, my Higher Power simply is "The Great Mystery!" I love it.

A Change in Perception

Joshua H.

I awoke at 3:30 a.m. today. I instantly regretted it. Feelings of oneness with the universe tend to escape me this early in the morning.

I had stupidly forgotten to pack a rain coat for this trip, so had reluctantly borrowed my mom's. I find it difficult to feel masculine when borrowing my mother's clothes, and it's important to feel like a man when you are about to ascend a 14,000-foot mountain nestled within the Colorado Rockies on a questionably cloudy day. It is also important to not die from exposure when doing so. And so I opted for the passing moment of humiliation.

My father turned 63 a couple of weeks ago. As a birthday present, I flew out to meet him in Denver this week so that we could summit Longs Peak together.

When I was a child, my father took me on several trips to Longs Peak in an attempt to reach its summit — for us, an ever-elusive goal. I was never able to reach the top of the mountain due to the eventual onset of altitude sickness, which I would succumb to three-quarters of the way up the peak. Without question or complaint, we always turned around, a mere hour away from summiting.

Over the years, I have often felt that I let my dad down in this respect. But not this day. Today would be our day of reckoning.

About 15 minutes into the hike from the trail head, I began to question the wisdom of my birthday present. My father was 63; I was apparently really out of shape; and because neither of us lived in Denver (the "Mile High City") we were not acclimated to the altitude. Logistically speaking, I was less likely to summit this mountain today than when I was five.

But I also couldn't just turn around, mostly because I would look like an idiot — which I try to avoid. As the labour of our ascent became more and more pronounced, I mentioned off-handedly that this had always seemed a lot easier when I was a kid.

"Well," my dad said, "This is considered one of the hardest 14K hikes in Colorado. Frankly, I was surprised that you wanted to do this one and not an easier one."

Easier one ... ?

"Uh, I thought this was the easier one, and that's why you always brought me here." Dad stopped walking and looked over at me.

"No, I brought you here when you were that young because I figured if you were able to tackle one of the more difficult mountains, all the rest of them would be that much easier for you as you grew up."

~

Once, in my early recovery, after I had finished venting to my sponsor about how poor my father's parenting skills were, he calmly suggested that I might want to explore how I had possibly wasted a lot of time lamenting how my father never seemed to understand me when in reality I had made little or no effort to try to understand who he was.

I was of course deeply offended by my sponsor's audacity in suggesting this, but instead decided to act like I agreed with this possibility. Not much later, I honestly began the work of finding out whether or not what my sponsor said was true. Unsurprisingly, it was.

~

I often found myself quite fearful of the idea of spirituality. This fear tended to look a lot like cynicism and distrust. In reality, I just didn't understand it all. Spirituality seemed like this overly vague idea with little or no modern-day application.

Over the years, I've come to find that spirituality is the means of awakening to the God that resides within me and acknowledging that same presence in others. This is by no means an easy task, so it is not surprising to me that I had spent so long avoiding and denying it. I mean, who really wants to acknowledge that the same Light that exists in me also exists in the person I feel has wronged me?

What I didn't know at that time years ago, when I began to make the first conscious efforts to understand my father, was that associatively I was also awakening to a spiritual way of living. Ultimately, spirituality for me is not some vaguely esoteric way of life; it is eminently useful. It is directly related to how I perceive and treat the people around me, both the ones I love and — perhaps even more so — the ones I'm not so thrilled about.

~

When my dad and I reached what is called the Keyhole, we had to turn back because of an impending electrical storm. I was both disappointed and mildly relieved. (Vomiting in public kind of embarrasses me and I was starting to feel the effects of altitude sickness.) We had once again made it to a point only a mere hour away from the summit.

As we began the descent back down, my dad smiled and said loudly, "Well, that was just great!" I could tell he really meant it. Without thinking, I replied, "You know, I always felt a little ashamed that I let you down and was never able to summit the peak."

He turned and said, "It was never about reaching the summit; I just wanted to spend time with you."

A Three-Headed Dragon with Ears Like Dumbo's on a Bicycle

Leslie H. (Munro 2003)

A crazy title, yes, but I promise I'll try to tie it all together for you. Here are some of my thoughts on balance in recovery. Please keep an open mind ...

Physical Balance: First Things First

Like the example of the Three-Headed Dragon we learn about in treatment at Renascent, I gain a measure of physical balance when I stop drinking and other drugging. Today, daily maintenance and improvement in physical balance for me includes working to reduce H.A.L.T. (Hungry Angry Lonely Tired) triggers in my day-to-day life. Balance here includes prayer and meditation around persistent bad habits. It means letting go of perfectionist, all-or-nothing thinking while challenging myself to improve. Balance improves with gratitude lists.

I sometimes think of the AA beam as the balance beam in gym. It takes practice and coaching and more practice to become an accomplished gymnast. I can't walk the AA beam when I'm exhausted or not eating or exercising properly. One day at a time, I gather physical balance and learn what it is like to walk with sober legs.

Emotional Balance & Easy Does It

Emotional benders, I have come to know, are every bit as deadly as my alcoholic ones. For me, gaining emotional stability and balance is a matter of repetition for emphasis: Don't drink or pick up, go to meetings, get a sponsor, call my sponsor, get active, get into service. I once heard a member of this fellowship say, "I said to myself at the beginning that eventually I would discover 'their' magic formula. After about 17 years, I finally figured it out. It's this: don't drink or pick up, go to meetings, get a sponsor, call my sponsor, get active, get into service — and pray like a ... [pray fervently and persistently]."

Spiritual Balance: Two Ears & An Open Mind

Where do we begin when we talk about this beautiful, spiritual program? I am reminded that the best beginnings usually come from listening ... deeply, regularly and thirstily. The old saying that I am given two ears and one mouth applies to me as an alcoholic and an addict.

An open mind is so precious. I came into recovery as an intolerant and morally arrogant person; one who didn't know that religion and spirituality can be two very different things. I actively sought out those who appeared to enjoy (imagine that!) their clean and sober lives and peppered them with questions. I began to get honest with myself and to share what was inside me with others in recovery. As a result, I learned what I believe to be two amazing truths, and these have set me free. One is that God is not limited by my understanding of God. The other? *There is no breaking point with God.*

Recovery Takes Time — And So Does Balance

At the website for Alcoholics Anonymous, www.aa.org, under the heading, "How Does AA Work?" I am reminded that recovery takes time. This truth is a key aspect of balance for me. It took me exactly 36 years from the day of my first drunk to the day when I was given a moment of clarity to see that I am an alcoholic, that I need help and where to find that help. I cannot get well overnight.

I Have the T-Shirt

Some years ago my children bought me a T-shirt that says in big, bold letters: "I KNOW I'M NOT PERFECT BUT I'M SO CLOSE IT SCARES ME." I treasure that T-shirt still and am learning to cherish the abundant opportunities my Higher Power gives me to laugh at myself.

I am not an engineer but I have it on good authority that balance involves a bicycle and requires two things: 1) putting both hands on the handlebars of discipline and 2) forward movement. So, if you see a funny looking, three-headed dragon with enormous elephant ears wearing a T-shirt with big, bold letters ... it might be me, pedalling like crazy, aiming for the future ahead ... and loving the thought that you're there beside me.

We're chatting as we go, marvelling that in this program balance comes from a seemingly contrary thing — that momentum carries with it the invitation to "pause, ask for quiet, and in the stillness simply say: 'God grant me the serenity to accept the things I cannot change, courage to change the things I can, and wisdom to know the difference. Thy will, not mine, be done.'"

Imagine!

Buddhism — The Spiritual Path That Fits

Mike R.

Some 10 years ago, I started to practice Buddhist meditation and study Buddhism in depth.

With 14 years of sobriety and having gone through the Steps 14 times, I felt I needed to be able to look at myself through a different lens. For me, this was the spiritual path that fit.

This is how my practice of the Four Noble Truths and the Eightfold Path of Buddhism works with my practice of the Twelve Steps.

The First and Second of the Noble Truths can be aligned with Step One.

Step One: We admitted we were powerless over _____ and that our lives had become unmanageable.

The First Noble Truth: Suffering human beings are subject to desires and cravings, but even when we are able to satisfy these desires, the satisfaction is only temporary. Pleasure does not last; or if it does, it becomes monotonous. Even when we are not suffering from outward causes like illness or bereavement, we are unfulfilled, unsatisfied. This is the truth of suffering.

The Second Noble Truth: The truth of the cause of suffering. The Buddha taught that the root of all suffering is desire, *tanhā*. This comes in three forms: greed and desire; ignorance or delusion; hatred and destructive urges.

In the First Noble Truth, I can see how drinking worked for a time, how it eliminated my internal suffering (restless, irritable, discontent). In the Second Noble Truth, I can see that suffering brings back the desire (obsession) to use or drink so I can fix the malady; that delusion can be twofold: 1) I don't have a problem and believe deeply that I don't and 2) This substance is doing something to relieve the malady and, of course, that greed is the selfishness in me.

93

The Third Noble Truth can be seen within Step Two.

Step Two: Came to believe that a power greater than ourselves could restore us to sanity.

The Third Noble Truth: Cessation of suffering. The Buddha taught that the way to extinguish desire, which causes suffering, is to liberate oneself from attachment. This is the Third Noble Truth — the possibility of liberation.

To liberate myself from attachment is to understand that lack of power is my dilemma and to come to believe that on my own, I am unable to relieve my addiction. So, there will need to be something greater than self.

The Fourth Noble Truth works with Step Three.

Step Three: Made a decision to turn our will and our lives over to the care of God *as we understood Him*.

The Fourth Noble Truth: Path to the cessation of suffering. This is the Buddha's prescription for the end of suffering: a set of principles called the Eightfold Path. The Eightfold Path is also called the Middle Way: it avoids both indulgence and severe asceticism, neither of which the Buddha found helpful in his search for enlightenment.

Step Three says *as we understood him*, not as others understand him. Here I am going to find my truth. But I need to remember it's not me. Also, the decision in this Step is just to move forward to find my truth and to follow the Eightfold Path.

The Eightfold Path

The eight stages are not to be taken in order, but rather support and reinforce each other.

1. Right Understanding: Accepting Buddhist teachings. (The Buddha never intended his followers to believe his teachings blindly, but to practice them and judge for themselves whether they were true.)

2. Right Intention: Committing to cultivate the right attitudes.

3. Right Speech: Speaking truthfully; avoiding slander, gossip and abusive speech.

4. Right Action: Behaving peacefully and harmoniously; refraining from stealing, killing and overindulging in sensual pleasure.

5. Right Livelihood: Avoiding making a living in ways that cause harm, such as exploiting people, killing animals, or trading in intoxicants or weapons.

6. Right Effort: Cultivating positive states of mind; freeing oneself from evil and unwholesome states and preventing them from arising in future.

7. Right Mindfulness: Developing awareness of the body, sensations, feelings and states of mind.

8. Right Concentration: Developing the mental focus necessary for this awareness.

Steps Four, Five, Six and Seven are essential to get to the practice of the Eightfold Path. Steps Four and Five assist me in finding where I was wrong in all eight areas of my life. I no longer do a column inventory, but inventory by putting my life against the Four Noble Truths and the Eightfold Path. Step Six is being willing to make the changes required for contented sobriety. Step Seven is being willing to let go of self, so these changes can take place.

I have to make the *Step Eight* list in order to be able to follow the path, and need to make my *Step Nine* amends because freedom is essential for my recovery.

Steps Ten and Eleven are strict disciplines and I must use them the way they were written. I am still human and make mistakes, and must rectify them promptly if I am to follow the path. At least each morning and night I go to the mat for meditation and prayer. (In Tibetan, the word Om or Aum is used to start and end prayer.) At night, I also do a daily review. Without meditation and daily review, I can return to the unconscious state where ego rebuilds, and it can take me out of the path I have chosen to follow.

This leads to the *Twelfth Step*. Carrying the message is essential to my sobriety, and the practice of the principles are the principles of the Eightfold Path. As for the spiritual awakening, there is a Zen saying: "Before enlightenment, chop wood and carry water. After enlightenment, chop wood and carry water." It tells me that no matter what, I must practice daily.

A God of My Understanding

Aruna A.

When we enter the world of recovery, we are in a sense reborn. During this process, many of us find a need to recreate our concept of a higher power, or to build upon the remnants of an existing faith. How and what encompasses a Higher Power? And in what way must one's faith adhere to the structure of the program of Alcoholics Anonymous?

I'd like to, if I may, share my experience on this topic. I'm originally from India and hail from an orthodox caste known as Brahmins, a class of Hindu priests and religious scholars. My family is traditional and religious in a gentle way.

In my childhood years, a sense of confidence in his faith allowed my father to encourage me to read great books of religion. He urged that I not compare, but rather find unity in the essence of all great faiths. At the same time, my parents demonstrated Hindu traditions and philosophies by example. Years later, this subtle approach would prove to be my saving grace.

I had some very profound realizations in early sobriety. I noted how very Christian the program of AA was. The format, fellowship, collecting money in baskets, coffee afterwards, all contributed to this. Temple services had none of these dynamics. I suppose Hinduism is a very autonomous faith and a need for community is attained largely through the extended family. While I was infinitely more comfortable with the latter, I tapped into my upbringing and "kept an open mind." The Lord's Prayer was another challenge; however, I choose to see this prayer as generous and all-encompassing, guiding me through the day's hardships.

Another obstacle was the concept of "Thy will, not mine, be done," which is very much the antithesis of the Hindu prayer. Hindus specifically pray for one's wishes to be heard. We are encouraged to put our intention out to the universe to give confidence to its manifestation. My struggle with adjusting to this difference within the two cultures prompted a desire to delve deeper into the intricacies of my religion. As I studied prayer and intention, I unearthed concepts in the Law of Detachment. I continued to put my intention out to the universe but detached from the results. I grew to trust that my prayers were indeed answered, regardless of the shape of their manifestation.

Contrary to popular belief, Hinduism is a monotheistic religion. The confusion lies in our philosophy and adaptation of a belief that God is everywhere and in everything: Creation — Brahma; Abundance — Lakshmi; Preservation — Vishnu; Destruction — Shiva; Loyalty — Rama & Sita. The list is vast and complex but the approach is simple in that it helps one comprehend God's omnipresence. A favourite of mine is Ganesh — the Remover of Obstacles. In sobriety I've found much comfort in praying to this "God."

Incorporating my faith was a difficult process but I learned more about my religion and was better able to practice the principles of AA to ensure sobriety. It was a worthwhile effort as my willingness was soon rewarded with occasional but profound experiences with God.

At four months sober, I recall having a magnificent moment of clarity while reading the Steps posted on a wall. Except for Step One, where we admit we are alcoholics and our lives have become unmanageable, I realized that the remaining 11 Steps embody the very philosophy that my forefathers and the pillars of my community adhered to as a way of life. Relief and a sense of safety overcame me. Despite years of spiritual turmoil, which alcoholics know too well, I had found the path homeward.

I once heard that the one thing all alcoholics have in common is that they've longed for God. I love that. Today, after years of being lost, I have a deep and unyielding faith in a God that I've always searched for. I believe it's the same faith that my ancestors experienced.

In Hinduism, it is said that all roads to Nirvana, or Spiritual Actualization, can be reached only through a vehicle — a golden chariot that comes in the form of a saint, guru, teacher or philosophy. Given the constraints of our Self, one cannot attain that state unaccompanied. It's amazing to me that the vehicle has come to me — a Hindu Brahmin woman — in the form of the program of Alcoholics Anonymous.

I believe now that the program of Alcoholics Anonymous and its Twelve Steps are divinely inspired. I thank God for bringing me to Alcoholics Anonymous, but mostly I thank Alcoholics Anonymous for bringing me to God.

Awakening the Spirit — Again … and Again … and Again …

George Z.

As I sit here and write this, the sun streams through my window on an intermittent basis, and when it does, I feel the warmth of its rays as joyously as I did on a summer day frolicking on the shore of Lake Superior as a little boy. I revel in this little blessing because today is a cool, windy, fall day with scattered clouds that allow the sun through only when there is proper alignment with my little piece of earth and space enough for the sun to peek through.

This could be a metaphor for spiritual awakening, and seems to me to be an apt description of what the perseverance of a real spiritual path is all about. Not so much about "doing" but about waiting to be found by the light of our own lives.

I have heard over and over that we are what we seek, and wherever we go there we are! So no matter how far we run or how much we avoid or how often we seek truth in other ways, we can find it only by facing ourselves as we are and where we are in the reality of our current circumstances.

It has taken me a long time to see this clearly — many years of sobriety and lots of years of life, and I am just beginning again! But really that seems to be the secret; to recognize we always begin again and never graduate, needing to learn things over and over.

What I have learned along the way is that all things that are really profound are also really simple: don't drink just for today, you can't give what you haven't got, you can't be anyone other than who you are. So often on my path, I have tried to be someone else, tried to be further along the path than I was, and tried to give what I hadn't truly integrated.

Always I was forced by the grace of God to see myself again and again as needing more healing, more growth and more love. Fear, anger, self-centredness and pride have been the clouds that block out the sun in my life. Humility (sometimes humiliation through my mistakes) and a willingness to learn again and again what I already thought I knew seem to be the prescription to take care of this illness of soul; this longing for wholeness and love.

Nowhere have my progress and pain, mistakes and metamorphoses been as evident as in my relationships, especially with my immediate family, my wife, children and siblings, and also with my co-workers and friends.

At best, these people show me how to be myself, through their acceptance, forgiveness, and love, even through the struggles and pitfalls of human experience with all its faults and failings, both my own and theirs.

At worst, I feel the effects of self-imposed loneliness and despair. Resentments, family feuds, arguments at work, severing of friendships, disappointment and loss — all of these point to one thing: How am I doing today with myself, with God and with the world around me? Am I relaxed and alert, moving through life lightly and freely? Or am I hanging on to everything and being distracted by all the confusion I create?

I have travelled far and wide. I've gone to many retreats. I've read hundreds of books. I've made heroes out of other people. I seemed to always avoid facing my own pain by overcompensating with more meetings, more friends, more trips, more things to do. Most of these things were not bad in themselves but they didn't help me to face myself as I had to when I came to the rooms of AA beaten by my addiction.

There have been many times in my sobriety where once again I have been beaten by the more subtle forms of my addiction, to approval, appreciation, work, stress, self-concern and avoiding. Usually some calamity or broken relationship caused me to face the real problem, ME!

These unresolved emotional programs — that helped keep me functioning during a chaotic childhood and messed-up teenage years, in active alcoholism, and even into sobriety — would not work anymore. I realized that even when one gets sober, the alcoholism doesn't end. The patterns seem to be imprinted on my brain. My heart is scarred by the wounds and unable to fully open.

My spiritual awakening has been a process, sometimes long and slow and painful, sometimes exciting and freeing. Sometimes there have been "spiritual experiences" that gave great insight but didn't remain.

I have found it necessary to integrate these moments of clarity and stay on the journey through the daily practice of meditation, prayer, personal inventory, therapy, silence and a constant re-commitment to the priorities in my life. Always renewing my commitment not to run, but to face everything and continue with the stability of the principles of the Twelve Steps. Listening to God in others and finding transformation by living right in the fire of my daily life. Not seeking to escape or be anyone or anywhere else.

I have found that my world is almost perfect when I have a degree of acceptance, love, and forgiveness, both for myself and others. All the spiritual wisdom in and out of AA seems to say the same thing: we awaken to find the truth in or own hearts and know who we really are — divine beings having a human experience that we co-create with every choice we make.

The truth for me is that spiritual awakening is a process of opening my heart to the God of the present moment and the people closest to me; learning to become the love I seek. As one author put it, "Love is the annihilation of illusion," and maybe spiritual awakening is the same thing because that is what we seek most: love.

What I need most is to wake up from my dreams and see life in truth. Carl Jung once wrote to Bill Wilson that he thought AA's successful "formula" was *"spiritus contra spiritum,"* a spirit-filled life replacing the need for spirits (drugs and alcohol). Awakening to a life of love and service, that's the beginning and end for me today.

A Glimpse of Sky

Anne P. (Munro 2005)

Over the years, I have tried many forms of meditation: sitting, standing, moving, breathing, stretching, "omming," staring into flames, staring into an empty wine bottle. I never experienced the great spiritual revelation and enlightenment I thought I was supposed to and I figured meditation just didn't work for me.

It wasn't until I practiced Step Eleven that I discovered the value and purpose of meditation. I was relieved to learn that it is "essentially an individual adventure, something which each one of us works out in his [or her] own way," and that "the object is always the same: to improve our conscious contact with God, with his grace, wisdom, and love." For me, this has come to mean a simple calming of my mind to clear the path for prayer to my Higher Power.

I consider this analogy: I am gazing into a small pond, attempting to see (and understand) the beauty of the stones that lay on the bottom. If there is wind or rain, the surface distorts my view of the bottom. If I stare too intently into the pond, my own breath disturbs the surface. Instead of seeing the water as an integral part of the pond, I start to regard it as a hindrance. Certainly, there is no way to "move" the water. The only way to get a clear vision of the stones is to remain still, wait patiently and allow the water to settle. Meditation, for me, is creating that stillness, clearing the thoughts that obstruct my "view."

Sometimes I find it quite difficult to be clear and patient, so a couple of exercises help me. I wake up in the morning and, if my mind is filled with thoughts about the busy day ahead, I write them out immediately. I list things that are troubling me, problems that I foresee and tasks that must be accomplished. When I put my list away, I feel I have freed myself from some of the "wind and rain" and created some free space in my mind.

As suggested in Step Eleven, I often read the St. Francis Prayer as preparation for my meditation. Alternatively, I might read the passage on acceptance in the Big Book or one of the Steps from the Twelve and Twelve. I also might finger through my set of "sobriety beads"; each one designated with an attribute I want to embody: joy, laughter, beauty, hope, faith, courage and creativity.

My meditation begins with just one thought gleaned from my preparation. I meditate for 10 minutes (using an egg timer on my night table). I hear my roommate leaving for work, car horns outside my window, birds meeting for breakfast; these sounds are all present in my meditation. I am alone, however, with my Higher Power and together we wait for my pond to still.

Some mornings, it never does. Some mornings, I see only mud on the bottom. Some mornings, though, I am truly able to examine the stones. It is important for me to remember that there is no success or failure here. The practice allows me to more easily follow with my morning prayer, asking my Higher Power for knowledge of his will and the strength to carry that out.

When I return to my initial list of worries, the day ahead invariably seems more manageable. Throughout the day, I can meet stressful moments with a brief return to my meditation and "Thy will, not mine, be done." I have learned how "intensely practical" my morning meditations are. I realize that perfect meditation is not the goal; the goal is my "emotional balance" and meditation is merely a vehicle.

It has not been easy to maintain this routine but the rewards have been miraculous. When I look into my pond now, sometimes the surface is serene enough to offer me a glimpse of sky.

Something on the Inside

Joe S.

I am First Nations of the Algonquin Wolf Lake Band. I am very proud of my heritage. This is the first part of spirituality — being proud of where I came from and of who I am. Another big part to me is that 2,000 years ago a Man came to earth and He taught us to love one another without conditions. This is spirituality at its finest — to love unconditionally.

I grew up in an alcoholic home with my brother and mother. My dad walked out on me at an early age. My brother was very violent. I didn't grow up on a reserve but in a little town in Quebec, Northwest of Ottawa. We were the only native people in that town. My mother, God love her, taught me about my native traditions as a young man. But I started drinking at an early age and did not hear any of it.

When I sobered up, I started to learn about my native culture and traditions such as the sacred medicines: tobacco, sage, cedar and sweet grass, and the seven grandfather teachings: honesty, love, humility, courage, respect, wisdom and truth. These are the same principles as in AA. Today I want these traditions to be a part of my life.

My last drink was on October 23, 1990 and I remember it like it was yesterday. I had my very first spiritual experience that night. Something happened to me that was very powerful. I looked around the bar I was in and I did not want to be there. I did not want to drink and I did not know how to stop. I was at a place of destiny with nowhere to turn but back to God. What a place to be.

I guess at that time you could have considered me an agnostic. God's Grace entered me for the first time in my life that night. What an unbelievable moment. I do not believe we know when we are going to take our last drink because if we knew, we would not need AA or treatment centres.

My second spiritual experience was when I came back to a meeting and again something happened to me. I felt the Grace of God in that meeting. I had been around AA since 1984 but had never surrendered. That night at the AA meeting, the word God was mentioned and my fists clenched and I got upset. I was agnostic then so God meant nothing to me. I wanted to leave but something on the inside of me told me to stay and listen.

An old timer at that meeting said something and the penny dropped for the first time in my life. I heard what I needed to save my life. He said to join a group, get a sponsor, get active in your home group and put the word God on the backburner for now. He said keep coming back until you come to believe in something that makes sense to you.

I could join a group and I could get a sponsor; this I could do. I did not know what to expect but I could deal with this. All I had to do was to get to meetings for now because there I knew I would be safe.

I got a sponsor and we got to work on the Steps. I started to come to believe in a Higher Power and I started to call that Higher Power God. Alcohol was my Power for a long time and now it was God and AA. I was praying every day, asking for help with my sobriety.

My wife started to trust me again. We have been together for 30 or more years now. I put my wife through hell when I was drinking. Today, I have a choice.

What does spirituality mean to me? Spirituality is a part of surrender. It is also being okay with who and what I am today. Spirituality is helping another human being with no thought of reward for myself. Spirituality is from within. To find your own Higher Power or spirituality, you need to wade through all sorts of different ideas and traditions to find what appeals to you, what you like and what makes you feel good. A genuine relationship with God — that is the true essence of Spirituality. God lives on the inside of me today.

God gave me my life back — that's His gift to me. When I help another alcoholic get sober, that's my gift back to God.

Seeing the Spirit in Others

Dale H. (Walker 1995)

In my drinking days, "kindness" was not a word in my lexicon. My emotional vocabulary included words like "judgment," "retaliation," "mistrust," and "so what?" And in the 38 long years it took me to walk through the doors of Renascent and AA, I never once heard of the concept of "love in action."

My alcoholic world was all about me. In my world, no one cared about me, so I cared about no one — except as they related to me and my wants and needs. I was actually proud of the fact that I was harshly judgmental of others. My mantra was, "Sure, I'm tough on other people, but I'm even tougher on myself!" as if this were a badge of honour.

And it was true. I held others up to impossibly high standards, so they would inevitably let me down and I could say to myself "See? I was right!" and drink to numb that tiny little part of me that had actually been hoping this time might be different. And every time I fell short of my own expectations, it would just be more proof that I was not good enough — a fraud, an imposter — and I would drink to numb the pain.

So when I first entered the world of AA, 28 days sober after my stay at Renascent, and was treated with kindness, love and a complete lack of moral judgment, I simply didn't know how to react. The moral high ground (or low ground) that for so long had been my foundation had shifted. I had lost my emotional footing. I didn't know anything, except that I was terrified to drink — so terrified that I did exactly what was suggested I do.

One of those suggestions was to volunteer for group service, so I dutifully signed up for kitchen duty, serving coffee. That was just the start of many years of service — at the group, at Intergroup, with General Service, with Renascent, with sponsees. Along the way — especially after doing my first Fourth Step — I discovered how my life had been completely run by absolute self-interest based solely on fear in all of its manifestations.

Recovery did a complete 180 on the way I viewed the world and my part in it. I began to think about what I could give, instead of what I could get. I began to see other people (and not only those in AA) as human beings, each with their own burdens to carry. It wasn't all about me. I started to see the guy who cut me off in traffic as just a human being who felt separate from the rest of us; the person who bumped into me on the street, scowling, as a human being who was stressed out, under pressures I would never know about. I stopped taking everything so personally. And I now have my own standards of behaviour. I'm not going to let the behaviour of others dictate how I respond to them.

My understanding of my Higher Power is described in Appendix II of the Big Book: "an unsuspected inner resource." I believe that this is our spirit, which is awakened when we do the Twelve Steps; that every human being has this spirit and that it's through this spirit that we connect to each other in a meaningful, compassionate and loving way.

A couple of years ago, I volunteered to sit on a committee at my group. The committee chair was a fellow who was probably the most difficult member of our group. During our first committee meeting, he was rude to me the entire time. After the meeting, I was so upset, I sat on the stairs outside and cried.

My sponsor magically appeared (how do they do that?) and I told her what had happened; that I didn't need this kind of crap at AA and I was thinking of quitting. She suggested that I try it again and this time before the meeting started say a prayer and ask that I be shown the God present in this man.

When I followed her suggestion at the next committee meeting, I had a completely different experience. I was aware of the spirit within him and of his humanity. And whether through my new vision of him, or his own realization of his past behaviour, he was never as difficult to deal with as on that first night. Years later, he still is who he is, but now I can see past the exterior and treat him as a fellow in spirit.

Being able to see the spirit in others makes it easier to demonstrate love in action. It's easiest, of course, to do this with strangers, and hardest to do this with those closest to us. But I have learned in AA (and through a series of disastrous relationships!) that love is truly a verb, not a noun — an action, not a descriptor.

To say "I love you" is easy, but ultimately meaningless unless it is demonstrated by our actions. And if my actions aren't coming from a place of love, I know there's something not right with my spiritual condition and I need to do some work to get back into balance.

At this point in my recovery, I'm glad to say that I no longer feel the need to judge others harshly. I'm still working on the self-judgment. I hope one day I'll be able to honestly and freely show myself the kindness and compassion I can now so easily show others. Let's just say I'm a work "in progress"!

What I Believe to Be True

Joe C.

Today, 36 years into my sobriety, I don't stay sober predicated on the existence of an intervening/interfering deity in my sobriety or in the world around me. I am not claiming the non-existence of God; I conduct myself and work the Steps as if God is mythical, because that is what is true for me. I find that the Twelve Steps offer the same life-altering force for my atheistic sobriety as they offer believers. I simply had to translate the theistic Twelve Steps into my language — not unlike what the French or Tibetan alcoholic must do.

I was told to keep an open mind; that remains to be good advice. I was told to "fake it until you make it" and that has shown to be a dangerous idea for me. Some of us just can't tell little white lies without tragic consequences. I wanted to feel like I belonged in AA, once I decided I did belong. I got the impression that belonging and believing in God were synonymous. I wanted so desperately to belong that I feigned God-consciousness. We addicts and alcoholics are good liars; talking the talk can go undetected for years. But living a lie is a ticking time bomb. And feeling inauthentic gets harder — not easier — as you go forward in recovery.

I meditated on and was open-minded to feeling a connection with Divine intervention. When I felt like I didn't get this God-stuff and everyone else did, I felt like an impostor, trapped in a catch-22. To be accepted for who I am, I would have to come out of my atheist closet. To fess up might excommunicate me, disconnecting me from my sobriety-maintaining bond of the AA fellowship. I paid close attention to how candid atheists were treated and talked about behind their back. I've experienced hostility at worst and a condescending attitude at best from some of AA's most outspoken believers.

While I was biding my time, the internet broke the deadlock. Being connected to members of the recovery community all around the world, I found that I was not alone. Being a sober skeptic was as legitimate as being an orthodox believer. Becoming part of a community within a community gave me strength and courage, and the catch-22 was broken. I felt more a part of AA being candid than massaging my language to sound like I fit in. I don't feel like I am missing something or that I need to be fixed. My belief in a world without a deity is far from conformity with the majority. But I feel equal. Non-believers aren't second-rate AA members. We are different, yet equal.

I had to get on to recovery through the Twelve Steps without a white-light experience and I found that in doing so, with an open mind, not believing in God was irrelevant to my recovery. I don't deny that a belief that God is doing for them what they cannot do for themselves is keeping many of my fellow AAs sober. But their belief in such a thing is no proof to me that it exists.

Today, I call myself an apa-theist. What that means is I don't know and I don't care. If the myth-busters disproved God or if God revealed Himself to us — whichever way it went — I wouldn't change how I conduct myself today or tomorrow. I live by values today that I expect any deity would approve of and in the absence of a watchful, punishing, nurturing, divine parent, my values are still the best way to live life — for me.

I have worked with countless alcoholics and I find that we don't "come to belief." It is my experience that we can no more change our belief than we can change our eye colour. We can come to understand what we do believe (what is true for us) and we can work the Steps in a way that works for us. Don't tell me that the only way to work the Steps is word for word. My experience suggests something very different. If you are working with a new member and a word is a deal breaker, change the word — the word won't mind. On page 63 of the Big Book, Bill Wilson talks about Step Three. "The wording was, of course, quite optional so long as we expressed the idea, voicing it without reservation."

Humanists, cognitive behavioural therapists, Aboriginal North Americans, Buddhists and atheists have all translated the Twelve Steps into a language that offers the alcoholic sobriety with integrity — not having to accept someone else's belief, and not having to deny their own.

Change My Feelings in a Heartbeat

MJ (Munro 2011)

Music can have the power for one to be healed...
It can create a portal for feelings to be revealed...
Has the power to transform every emotion...
Bring you from the depths of despair to the waves of a beautiful ocean.

Can be used to enhance a beautiful state...
To feed resentment and perhaps fuel more hate...
To wallow in sadness and create even more...
Or to switch it up and dance till you're sore!

It can feed my disease of perception if I guide it to be so...
However, now that I'm more aware... and the truth I know...
I have to face that I have choices between play and pause...
As the music I listen to is the symptom, not the cause.

Music has always played a very important and beautiful role in my life. I've been blessed to have this grow and expand in wonderful ways throughout my recovery so far, whether it be for pleasure, healing, reflection, romance, meditation or plain old fun!

It can change my feelings in a heartbeat.
You can't stop me from smiling when you throw in that drumbeat.
My responsibility lies in the choices I make.
Whether that be listening to certain music, or the substances I do or do not intake.

I always gravitated towards music as an expression of myself and, in particular, as a way to deal with difficult emotions. Well, perhaps sometimes to "wallow in" or "feed and help painful feelings grow"! I also intuitively used it for good and healing, but I didn't know how to gauge this as I do now.

I love music and one of the incredible gifts I've been given is the ability to create some music of my own. Playing the piano for hours or listening to albums has also been very therapeutic and fun — whether done solo or in a beautiful bonding experience with my family and friends.

What I now realize in my recovery is the responsibility I have to do the next right thing in order to stay in a place of physical, mental, emotional and spiritual health. Part of this is "listening to the next right song."

I think there are times when certain music can be a good thing. When someone I love died, I listened to some very sad music for quite some time. I believe that for a period of time it was healthy for me to sort of stay in that place, to stay in the grief and possibly even feed it with this music. It helped heal me in its own way. However, there did come a point where it did not serve me or my recovery to listen to those songs, and to do so would have kept me in emotions and feelings that would have been detrimental to my recovery.

I am now able to ask myself when I find myself spiraling into states of being that are painful: Do you want to keep feeling depressed? Or do you want to feel _____? And then I have a choice. I can choose to listen to music that feeds the pain or music that switches it up and places me in a different state of mind and being.

I think so much can be written about the power of music. This bit of writing has only barely scratched the surface. It plays a part in my daily life to a profound degree. It is infiltrating my being in ways I never could have imagined, and I am enjoying exploring and experimenting with it every step of the way. I hope you are enjoying your journey with music as well!

Wishing you a beautiful day!

We Share So Much

Nasser S.

There are over 30,000 AA members living in Tehran. This is not an underground movement, as the priests or mullahs run the country and are the gatekeepers of all books that enter Iran. The Big Book, because it is compatible with the principles of the Koran, is not only allowed but actively supported the government.

So for me as a Mosalman, it was not difficult to embrace AA once introduced to it. A Mosalman is a person who has completely surrendered to Khoda (Farsi word for God) or who has completed Step One.

The Koran says, "I like the people who are honest, patient, do good deeds and pass on what is given." These are AA beliefs. The Koran begins with the option of who wants to live a life of virtue — it's a choice just like recovery. Prayer and meditation are very much part of being a Moslem — Step Eleven. When you drill down to core spiritual concepts, there are many similarities. We all pray to the same God — we just call it different names.

For me, the key differences revolve around suggestions (Big Book) versus orders (Koran) and differing approaches to punishment. In AA, there is no punishment but instead equal forgiveness. For a Moslem, it is best to forgive but if forgiveness isn't granted, punishment is specific and must be exactly proportionate to the sin. However, both AA and the Moslem faith subscribe to making amends and similarly only when it doesn't injure someone in the process.

Before joining AA 11 plus years ago, I was a part-time Moslem. I wasn't very involved. Joining AA has allowed me to deepen my Moslem faith. But I find that the AA traditions influence my attitudes and level of involvement. While I do work within the community and through the mosque, I do not want to hold any special positions. I prefer the democratic and more humble nature of AA. I don't like politics and I don't like anything that gives one person more status. I don't like bosses.

These are some of the reasons why I find AA so comfortable. I prefer to see a sermon in action rather than hear one. I relate more to the people in AA who are authentically engaged in practicing honesty, caring, patience and forgiveness. There is no room for justification in AA. Your recovery demands absolute honesty and the rigorous practice of spiritual principles.

So I go to a church on Wednesdays and a mosque on Thursdays — both work in my life even though not everybody understands it.

Twenty-one years ago, a Farsi author living in Los Angeles translated the Big Book and then returned to Iran to carry the message. In Toronto, I don't see a lot of Moslems at AA meetings. Like me, not every Moslem is able to adhere to the Koran's prescription not to drink and gamble, and so it's safe to say there are lots of Moslems suffering.

I ask myself why Moslems don't turn to AA in Toronto as they do in Iran. I think it's because no one in the community knows about AA in Toronto. If more people knew and went, more would join them and feel comfortable. There are advertisements for methadone clinics in Moslem newspapers but none for AA or centres like Renascent. Because they serve a single purpose, AA meetings are not allowed in Mosques (in Iran, meetings are held in municipal spaces). I was taken to my first meeting through a shelter — I was told to just do it.

Language and culture are other barriers. God willing, I would like to start a Farsi-language meeting in the Bayview and Steeles area. Perhaps this would be a good first step in helping fellow suffering Moslems.

An Agnostic's Journey

Jason A. (Sullivan 2006)

I couldn't believe it — here I was, a card-carrying agnostic, about to step into a world of spiritual growth. How did I get myself into this?

Let me back up a few years. Like many alcoholics, my self-centred pride, ego and fear, combined with copious amounts of booze, had taken me to the brink of a life-changing situation. My wife was leaving with the children.

In desperation, I tried an AA meeting one Sunday night, and generally liked what I saw and heard, except for that dreaded "G" word that we hear so much in a 12-step program of recovery. I recoiled from it as if from a hot flame. My mind closed to the idea that I needed help from "God." What followed was a year of dragging along a bottom that I refused to admit I had hit.

Don't get me wrong, I understood what the concept of a God was. As a youth, I was fascinated by the Gods of the ancient Greeks and Romans, of the Egyptians and the Indians. But as a man of science, I chalked up all of those beliefs to ignorance on the part of the people who held them. If they didn't understand something, they blamed one God or praised another. In my arrogance, I believed that there was no mystery that mankind and science wouldn't someday reveal or explain.

That kind of thinking carried through to the day I entered treatment at Renascent. One simple phrase from a counsellor there changed my thinking: "All your best thinking got you right here today." That night I stared out my window and thought of all the things that were more powerful than I was, asked a God I didn't believe in for help, and my eyes opened to a world I never realized was there.

When I took away my preconceived notion of God as a judge, jury and executioner, and instead pictured the forces of nature, I slowly started to understand what a Higher Power could be to me. All I knew for sure was that the constant itch, that all-consuming and often overwhelming desire to drink, was gone. And since that day I've grown and developed a stronger sense of what my spirituality means to me and how I relate to the world around me.

Every Step I worked on in the Big Book took humility and for me to surrender as I began. And the work I did on each Step resulted in a deeper connection to God as I understood it.

While I was working on the Steps, I started collecting phrases and messages from speakers with a spiritual theme. I've attended a number of weekend retreats where I could explore and advance my spiritual journey. And I also keep lots of books and other readings dealing with spiritual awakening close by.

Sometimes I am preoccupied with the "why" of it all — why does this work, why can everyone do it slightly differently, why can some people seemingly not get it at all and still stay sober? And I found out the only real answer to those "whys" is, "It doesn't really matter!"

When it comes to nurturing and developing my own sense of the spirit, I tend to read and explore a number of different belief systems and teachings from all over the world. Far Eastern philosophies, Native spiritualism, Mexican native teachings, modern thinkers — they all have had an influence on my connection to a Higher Power. I could pick just one thing and learn to be happy.

I've learned that most, if not all, carry the same message. And it's probably most familiar in the form of the Golden Rule: Do unto others as you would have done unto you. Very simple, but not always easy because it works in many ways; not just in harm done to others, but in the gifts you receive as well.

Another powerful idea is that "God is Love, and Love is God." When we love each other, we wish each other the best and don't cause any pain we wouldn't be willing to endure ourselves. What a lot of people don't realize is that there's a limitless supply of it to give away. If someone rejects that love out of selfishness or self-righteousness, it's not gone — God's always got more for you and me to give.

By keeping the principles of the Twelve Steps in mind as I go about my business, and striving to learn something new each day about myself, the world around me, or the mysterious force that unites us all, my connection to my Higher Power constantly grows.

So far, my path to enlightenment has brought me a long way from where I started, and I hope not to see the end of it for a long, long time. My understanding of it, my conscious contact with God as it were, will be as deep as I want it to be.

It's been quite a journey from my agnostic beginnings, and I look forward to the continuing journey ahead.

The Tiny Voice Inside

Mary C. (Munro 2003)

When I started to write this article, I went to my old friend, the paperback dictionary, and found the definition of spiritual: "of the spirit or soul, ie: person's essence or intelligence." This gave me my start.

When I think of spirituality, I think of the journey I have lived in developing my spirituality, as opposed to the traditional practices that I follow in my religion. When I came to AA, I encountered the concept of a Higher Power — only to discover that I had believed in a Higher Power all my life.

I was brought up in an English Roman Catholic family with strong values and regular attendance at church. Catholicism is my religion, but spirituality shapes the way I live and the way that God directs my life (when I listen).

I believe that my God is a God of Love who wants the very best for me. I also believe that God gives me freedom of choice. He/She allows me to make my own choices, which also means that I live with the consequences of these choices.

Spirituality for me is a way of life. My life today is a summary of choices that I have made or not made. I do not always have a choice in what shapes my life, but I do have a choice in how I respond to what comes my way. One of these choices is a decision to remain sober today and to live in today.

My parents chose to send me to a French Catholic school. This opened my mind to appreciate different cultures and thoughts, which I still benefit from today. My parents shared their religion with me. This gave me a religious base to build on and values that have helped me develop my spirituality, my way of life and to accept the Third Step. I do not take my belief in a Higher Power, whom I chose to call God, lightly.

I believe that I have been given a gift — my faith — but with it also comes a responsibility. I feel responsible for sharing this gift of mine, not in trying to convince others to find a religion, but in living my life in a way that deepens my own spirituality and hopefully brings a little more happiness and peace to others. I also strive for balance between my own co-dependency (putting other people's needs first) and taking care of myself. I live this struggle every day ... to find this harmony as I do to stay sober, one day at a time. Some days, the only thing that I can do is keep saying the Serenity Prayer over and over.

I meditate and do my readings most days and thank God for what I have been given in my life. Part of my journey has come from having been a nurse and, at another time, an assistant in a community with people who are my friends. Many of these people are seen in our society as being mentally challenged, but they have helped me deepen my belief in a God of my understanding.

I also have three wonderful children whom I know I hurt when I was drinking. I am regaining their trust and spending time with my three grandchildren who, hopefully, thanks to rehabs, AA programs and the help of God, will never see me drinking.

My husband and I have recently separated after 40 years of marriage (not my decision) and he would give my disease of alcoholism as the main reason. I am still trying to understand the "why" of his decision but I am gradually seeing that this is like the "why" of my alcoholism. The "why" is not important. My acceptance of the situation, without the reason, can be there only if I pray and turn it over to God.

My faith has taught me that God knows what is good for me and that I always learn through the difficult times. The difficulty for me is to continue to believe that God still carries me "in the palm of his hands" when the going is tough.

My sobriety and my faith are, for me, an ongoing challenge that I must work at "one day at a time" for the rest of my life. My faith journey tells me that when I take time to listen to that tiny voice inside me, God lets me know if I am on the right track or if I need to make adjustments. If I feel a deep peace within me, I know that all is right between me and my God. If I feel unsettled, anxious and troubled, I need to make some adjustments to lessen the distance I have created between myself and God.

My faith is based on action. God is always there for me. I have the responsibility to call my sponsor when I need help and I also need to call on God to help me. This is how my spirituality is based. My religion and my AA program give me guidance, but my spirituality is demonstrated by how I act out my life and for that, I am responsible.

This has helped me to accept my human-ness, to live life on life's terms, to stay sober and to each day be grateful for all the gifts I have received.

I also must remind myself that I'm on a path, a journey. I am not perfect and never will be. I have a lifetime to walk this path, one day at a time for the rest of my life.

Please remember that this is only a reflection of my journey.

I wish you a lifetime of sobriety, one day at a time.

Peace and Hope from Meditation

Paul M. (Sullivan 2002)

In addition to the anguish I was experiencing as a practicing alcoholic back in 2002, I was suffering from Limbic ADD as well as depression. My mind was, to say the least, not my own. Incapable of being in a restful state for more than a few minutes at best, my mind and body were completely expended of all useful and positive energy.

During the second week of treatment, I was introduced to the practice of meditation as a means of relaxation. Although I failed miserably, I developed an intense and immediate attraction for the concept, and today, 10 years later, I am using meditation on a daily basis as a means of stress reduction and as a means to enlightenment in my journey as a practitioner of Buddhism.

The Buddha is said to have identified two paramount mental qualities that arise from wholesome meditative practice; these being serenity and insight. What a coincidence! These were the same two qualities I had been searching for all my life. I had proven to myself time and time again that alcohol, weed and opiates were not the answer and only led to increased paranoia and confusion.

Given my state of mind at the time, knee deep in empty bottles and empty thoughts, I recognized that I needed to not only abstain from alcohol but also to actively adopt a way of life that would lead me closer to being the kind of man I wanted to be ... calmer, happier, more helpful to those around me. Meditation as part of my recovery was the answer.

Followers of Buddhism will tell you that the practice of meditation is the true entry into the Dharma realm (the path of righteousness, in simple terms). For me, meditation keeps me grounded and allows me to focus on the moment and to contemplate things as they are now.

When my addiction had me by the throat, I was led in whatever direction the wind was blowing — especially if the smell of alcohol was in the wind. Thousands of attempts at abstinence and self-improvement were dropped by the wayside when the winds of addiction were blowing.

Each shot of vodka led me to experience abject bouts of guilt at having once again abandoned the path I was trying to follow. Even after leaving the house, and for the first year of my new-found sobriety, my mind was right at home with a troop of Gibbon monkeys. Attending meetings and close contact with my higher power was keeping me sober but I needed more, something outside the program.

As simply as I can remember it happening, I woke up one day and sat cross-legged on the floor in the darkness of my bedroom facing the wall and closed my eyes for a few minutes. I was bombarded with thoughts and mind flashes but sat there anyway, allowing all these "mind bombs" to go off in my head. Surprisingly, after this session I felt a modicum of peace and, more importantly, hope. Mindful of the fact that I'm terrible at pursuing anything consistently and for any length of time (which makes my sobriety even more of a miracle), I have been setting aside time for meditation ever since, allowing of course for periodic failings.

Meditation, as I have come to learn, is hard work. It takes incredible discipline to train the mind and body in this tumultuous millennium that we all live in. "Feelings come and go like clouds in a windy sky. Conscious breathing is my anchor." So said the venerable Vietnamese Zen Buddhist monk Thich Nhat Hanh, and it aptly describes my attraction to meditation today. I need to re-centre myself and escape from the stinking thinking so prevalent in our addictive consciousness.

There are numerous ways to meditate, just as there are numerous positions in which to sit. I prefer to place a small cushion on a larger one (Zafu and Zabuton cushions) and to loosely cross my legs while placing my left hand in my right hand. Bowing my head towards my chest, I close my eyes and begin to count my breaths. If I lose count, I simply begin again. A common misconception with meditation is that you must block all thought from entering your mindful state.

This is not true. Allow the thoughts to enter, acknowledge them, then let them go.

I began sitting for 10 to 15 minutes a day then moved that to two sittings a day. Today, I sit in the late afternoon or evening for approximately an hour. I also enjoy walking meditation in the forest near my home and often meditate for a few minutes in public places if I need to, although that requires a great deal of concentration.

I believe that it's perfectly okay to change your practice from time to time. On one day, I may sit in silence; on another, I may listen to chants or music from Tibetan Buddhist monks such as the Gyuto Monks. Either way, meditation has worked for me. Give it a concerted effort and I think it can work for you too. Namaste.

Living Life to the Fullest

Karen B. (Munro 2012)

> *From sorrow comes great joy.*
>
> *Wisdom of Kahana*

The later years of my drinking and using fell very short of feeling joyous. What was once a release and problem solver had become a prison, physically and mentally. Using took away my ability to be present in the moment and to be aware of the good things going on around me.

I was a blackout drinker. Photographs over the years tricked me into thinking I must have had a good time. I was surrounded by smiling people in those images ... but I couldn't remember a thing! Later on, I was all alone in my using. No phone calls, no plans, no one to meet. I was lucky to get into the shower on some days. I couldn't sincerely appreciate anyone or anything around me. All I cared about was where the next drink or drug was coming from. In my twisted thinking, I thought that was all I really needed to be fulfilled. We alcoholics are no strangers to pain and lack of enjoyment.

So how did I get from that life to experiencing happiness, freedom and — dare I say — fun?

My journey into a life filled with joy started when I went to Renascent's Graham Munro Centre in July 2012. I had previously been to detox three times and to two other treatment centres, one of which was AA-based. But I didn't have the readiness to accept my disease, I wasn't connected to a higher power, I didn't believe in myself and I truly thought I could learn to moderate my drinking one day on my own. I finally learned the hard way, over and over, that I couldn't stop after my first drink.

At Renascent, I learned to open my mind to a God of my understanding. My counsellors told me that "it will get better" and "this too shall pass," and I believed them. I had difficulty at first. I did not want to wait for my issues to pass to feel better ... I wanted my unease gone now!

During my humble beginnings, I thought I would never find happiness and freedom in sobriety. I felt uneasy and couldn't tap into happy thoughts. But at Renascent ... finally! I became open, honest and willing. I had hit a bottom that scared me enough to hear what the counsellors had to say. What a blessing!

The women in the house started reading the Big Book, Alcoholics Anonymous. We attended regular meetings. I felt at peace when I was around people who understood what I was going through. What a powerful circumstance to be in ... I felt Grace. I came to love the meetings and to consider other members my close friends. The sisters I met at Renascent have continued to bring me joy and we exchange experiences that I learn from every day. I also found an amazing sponsor while I was at the house.

The "work" that everyone is always talking about (working the Twelve Steps) sounds intimidating, but try not to be scared. It's by truly working the Steps and learning about ourselves that serenity starts to set in. I don't know all the answers as to why this program works as well as it does, but I have stopped asking why. I don't need to anymore! I see it working for me every day and the people around me. I have faith.

Getting into AA (not just being around AA as I was before) gave me the ability to feel joy in sobriety. If I couldn't enjoy my sobriety and have fun with it, I don't know if I could stay sober. Happiness in sobriety is a choice. I am capable of choosing happiness now that my head is finally clear — and I have a strong community that keeps me that way. I can now focus on what people are saying to me — and there's a lot of fun to be had with honest sharing.

Today, I can enjoy many of the same freedoms as people who are not addicts. I am watching the promises come true for me. Doing the "work" is fun for me. I have so many "aha" moments every day.

I used to mistake chaos for excitement. In the first few months of recovery, I was mistaking serenity for boredom. But AA has given me the opportunity to have joy in the small victories in life. I have awareness of those things now: a great phone call, a walk with my dogs, a perfect sunny day and silly things that amuse me. Laughing at last! Real laughter at moments I wouldn't have even noticed when I was using.

I gave myself permission to say no to events and situations until I was ready. That really helped me to stay sober until I could invite more into my life. Now I can enjoy restaurants, patios, camping and dances. The list is endless. I have the ability to get excited about an upcoming event without feeling as though my sobriety is threatened. Added bonus ... I can remember every detail!

My higher power is always with me; I surround myself with my fellow alcoholics and addicts. I have leaped into the program with both feet! I love the new me and so do my family and friends. I have the freedom to let go of resentments and I can be truly happy, joyous and free. If you are new to Alcoholics Anonymous, be open, honest and willing learn and you will tap into your joy in sobriety!

HP Surfing

Jerome G.

These days, my relationship with a Higher Power can perhaps be best described by a surfing analogy. There is lots of effort required on my behalf to align myself properly. If I do, the results can be sublime. If I go against it, the results can be exhausting, discouraging or even disastrous.

To surf, I need to acquire equipment (proper clothing, board, safety harness) and get myself to an appropriate location. Once there, I walk down to the shoreline and try to spot where the waves are rising. Then I jump in. The shore break is hard to get past; it resists my even starting out. But I persist and soon am able to lie on the board and then must paddle hard to get out to the area I've spotted to catch a wave.

If I make it to the designated area, I then have to sit up on the board and watch out to sea in an effort to spot a promising swell. When I've done so, I turn and start to paddle like crazy to get up speed to catch the wave. If I manage to do so — an uncertain proposition at best — I then have to try to stand up. If I can do all that and am still on the wave, I have a chance of a ride. Often, the wave won't crest or will break in the wrong place or I'll just fall and I'll have to turn around and paddle back out. But, once in a while, I'll get a great ride!

Even then, I'll have to be careful. I may try to ride the wave too far and could get dashed on the rocks or scraped on the beach. Or I could get going fast and then tumble and crash and watch out that I don't drown. But, if my efforts align with the wave in the right way, I'll have a few moments of bliss where I'm one with the power of the water.

That's how I see Higher Power — like the power of the wave. If I put in the work and pay attention to the flow, I can go with it and be held. But many times I will fail. The more I practice, the better I'll get. I'll gain confidence and be able to face bigger challenges.

But there's another element to my experience of Higher Power that's not immediately obvious in this oceanic analogy, which seems primarily to be about my relationship with the physical world.

My deepest problems are not in relating to the universe but to other people. I started practicing my addictions because I felt unsafe with people — in fact, often secretly terrified. I liked the ease and comfort I felt with booze and drugs, and tried to gain your love and acceptance by convincing you how thin, successful, helpful and funny I was.

Early in recovery, I struggled with defining Higher Power. Slowly, I started to gather helpful clues. Step Twelve talked about practicing "these principles"; Tradition Two mentioned "a loving God"; Appendix II told me the essence of spirituality is "willingness, honesty and open mindedness."

I was asked what human traits, what principles, my Higher Power should comprise. Based on the traits I admire in other people, I chose things like kindness, fairness, forgiveness, loyalty and a sense of humour.

So, as the St. Francis Prayer (Step Eleven) suggests, it has become my responsibility to be a channel — a practitioner — of those traits. Do unto others as I would have them do unto me.

In essence, those principles have become my ocean, the power of the waves, my Higher Power in relationships with other people.

Before recovery, it was all based on what I wanted. I was motivated by fear, shame and loneliness and used all the tools at my command to bend the world to my liking. I was about as successful at that as I am trying to make a wave rise or change direction at my command!

Now, like the surfer setting out to find where the waves are breaking, I have to pay much more attention to the ebb and flow of social and community behaviour. I have found that the key to that is practicing the principles of a Higher Power. I can still try to influence the world around me, but have to be aware that I am much more likely to have a good ride if I am aligned with others rather than trying to bend them to my will.

I don't worry too much these days about knowing god's will for me — I'm here to have a human experience. But I pray often for the power and courage to practice love and to be of service, especially when I feel lonely and afraid. Sober and connected. What a ride!

Reaching My Own Personal Yom Kippur

Yasmin O.

Yom Kippur (Day of Atonement) is the holiest day of the year in the Jewish calendar. It follows 10 days after Rosh Hashanah, the Jewish New Year. According to the Sages, it is the day that God writes in his holy books what the coming year is going to look like for each and every person.

In the 10 days following Rosh Hashanah, called *Yamim Noraim*, it is believed that God opens the channels to the sky directly to allow any prayers and requests to go through his gates of Heaven. In these 10 days, Jewish people all around the world pray and ask for forgiveness and plead with God to "change His mind" if He wrote anything bad in his books for the coming year.

Yom Kippur is believed to be the day that God signs his books and the decisions for the upcoming year have been made. After Yom Kippur, the coming year's events have been decided by God — for better or worse. It is believed that a prayer on Yom Kippur, a day for self-exploration, is the most important prayer of them all.

The connection between Yom Kippur and recovery is, of course, the prayer. After all, we learn that every day in recovery is a day for self-exploration, every day is a day to turn our will to our Higher Power and every day is a day to ask for forgiveness.

During Yamim Noraim, we are expected to look at the year that has passed and make a list of all of our wrongdoings before asking for God's forgiveness of those sins. The custom is that you need to first ask forgiveness from God before you can ask forgiveness from others — just like in the Twelve Steps! Around Yom Kippur is when Jewish people around the world start making their amends to others.

Growing up in a Jewish Orthodox home back in Israel, the holiest place of them all, I felt resentment towards Yom Kippur. I used to think that Yom Kippur was when I was being judged by God for all my wrongdoings during my active addiction — the theft, the lies, the using, the cheating, the manipulating, the broken promises and everything horrible that my addiction caused me to do. I used to think, can it really be that easy? Fast for 24 hours, go to synagogue, say my prayers, ask for forgiveness and with a whip of a wand it'll all go away? Is there really nothing more to it? Surely it can't be that easy! How difficult would it be to go up to those so many people that I've hurt and say the words, "I'm sorry"?

It was only when I found this wonderful program that I realized that, yes, it is possible! That, yes, it wasn't me who was doing all those horrible things, it was my disease that took control over my actions, my thoughts and everything that is me. Slowly, I discovered that, yes, I can be forgiven! And, yes, the sins can be put to rest and, yes, there is a better way of life.

Yom Kippur has been very significant in my road to recovery. In Steps One through Three, I turned my will over to God and asked Him to accept me as I am and help to rebuild my personality. I slowly made a soul-searching inventory when I reached Step Four, confessed it to God and another person in Step Five and worked my way into Steps Six and Seven, where I did exactly what one would do on Yom Kippur — accept and forgive. Then I was finally ready to make my amends. I made a list in Step Eight of all the people I'd hurt and asked them to forgive me in Step Nine. Finally, I was clean. Finally, I had reached my own personal Yom Kippur.

One of the biggest traditions of Yom Kippur is to wear white, the colour of purity, and go to a natural source of water and dip your feet in it. The purpose of doing so is to "let go" of all the sins and be pure and ready to accept the New Year with all of its blessings and fresh beginnings.

On this Yom Kippur, I will be reminded of my past sins; those during my addiction and those of my recovery. I will yet again turn my will to Him and pray and ask for another clean year in recovery and another chance at life. I will dip my feet into the pure water and ask to let go of my sins from the past year and pray for a fresh start for the year to come.

I wish you all to reach your Yom Kippur when you are ready to do so, I wish you all to be able to reach that place of purity in your souls and, most of all, I wish you all to be honest with yourselves on your road to recovery, which is an everlasting journey.

When I Least Expected It ...

Richard T. (Sullivan 2008)

Thinking back on it now, I realize I had a "spiritual awakening" long before I knew what a spiritual awakening was.

My introduction to religion came when I was about five years old. I went to Sunday school and learned about God. But that was somebody else's concept of God, not mine. And as I grew older, I found myself drifting away from that God — mainly because I couldn't figure out what He was. I didn't think God was a guy sitting on a cloud "out there" somewhere, playing a harp. But what was He?

Then, one Saturday afternoon, it came to me. When I least expected it.

It occurred to me slowly, as I was watching a program on television about an Australian husband and wife doctor/nurse team who had been sent by the Australian government to help treat people in several villages along the coast of New Guinea or one of the (at the time) large but remote and sparsely inhabited jungle islands in the Pacific.

After making contact with these people, the Australians were told about a so-called "lost tribe," a group of people who were believed to be living far into the densely jungled interior and who might also require medical attention.

As they made their way farther and farther into the remote, almost impassable interior, the two Australians eventually did come upon a small group of extremely isolated, primitive people who, as far as the Australians could determine, had never come into contact with any other people. Ever.

Certainly, they had never seen white people before. They thought the Australians were "walking dead" and were terrified to go near them.

However, as the husband/wife team got to know the people better and became friends, they were able to "talk" to each other through a sign language they developed. During these "conversations," one of the things the Australians discovered was that these primitive people — who had never seen or been influenced by missionaries or by anyone or anything else — believed in a higher power or "great spirit" who lived up in the sky. And who benevolently provided all of their basic necessities or "daily bread," such as food, rain, sunshine and fertility. And good health.

At first, I thought, Isn't that a coincidence? Their belief in God is pretty much the same as mine was. But then, as I continued to think about it, I found myself wondering, If these completely isolated people had never talked with anyone from the outside world, how did they know about God? Who told them? Where did their belief in a higher power come from?

Maybe our understanding of God is instinctive. Or spiritual. Something that is born within us. I believe now that, even if I had been born on an isolated island, with no one else there to tell me anything about anything or influence my thinking in any way, I would naturally and instinctively have come to believe in a higher power myself.

That's when I had what I consider to be a spiritual awakening. In that moment, I realized that God exists within me, guiding me in all that I think and say and do. He's not up there in the sky somewhere.

He's right down here with me. A part of me.

Everything suddenly seemed to fall into place for me. I had never felt closer to God than I did at that moment. And have ever since.

I also feel that my life is largely predetermined, out of my hands, beyond my control. I'm like a leaf on a river. Just along for the ride.

It was quite an experience. And it's really quite amazing what you can learn from a bunch of people with bones through their ears.

St. Francis, My Mom and I

Dale H. (Walker 1995)

When I was newly sober, we read the St. Francis Prayer at a Step Eleven discussion meeting. My immediate reaction was "Well, it's a great prayer for a *saint* ..."

And then I did my first Fourth Step. My mom was the first name on my resentment list. I was convinced that she had never liked me, that I was a constant source of disappointment for her, that she relentlessly criticized my every move. I couldn't remember her even once telling me that she loved me. And I resented the hell out of her for it. We had started arguing when I was 13 and had never stopped. By the time I walked through the doors at Renascent, we had been estranged from each other for years.

But when I did that first Fourth Step, I was gifted with the understanding that all of my resentments were focused on "poor little me." Poor Dale — I never got enough attention, enough love, enough admiration, enough of anything! I had spent my entire life viewing everyone's actions through the prism of an infinite self-centredness that could never be satisfied. I was a bottomless well of need.

When I started to look at *my part* in the Fourth Step, I realized that I'd only ever seen my mother as an extension of me and my needs, never as her own person, as a human being with her own emotional life. I had only ever thought of what I was getting — or not getting — from her. I had never once thought about *giving of myself* to her — giving love, understanding, compassion ... anything. For most of my life, I had given her nothing but grief and worry.

I decided that I would put my ego aside and would simply try my best to just love her; not seek anything in return from her, for once, but just try to love her as much as I could. For once in my life, I would simply try to give rather than try to get.

I started calling home every Sunday, asking her how her week had been and actually listening to her and supporting her; feeling compassion for her when she encountered difficulty. Before each call, I would pray for the ability to talk to her from a place of love, not of ego. At the end of each call, I'd say "I love you, mom. Talk to you next week." She would respond with "Goodbye, dear" and that was just great by me.

I began visiting my parents more often. Before I arrived and each morning during my visit, I would pray the same prayer. If mom disagreed with me about something, I didn't pursue it. If she told me there was a better way to do something, I didn't argue. I either did it her way or my way, and let it go. And when I left, I would give her a hug and tell her I loved her. And she would say, "Goodbye, dear. Drive carefully." And that was just great by me.

I started feeling so much better about our relationship. I actually looked forward to talking to her and seeing her. I felt good just by being loving to her. I didn't seek or expect anything back; it was good enough to just give of myself, in love. This was completely new for me!

And then, after about a year of this practice, something miraculous happened. We were talking on the phone, and when I said "I love you, mom. Talk to you next week," she replied "I love you, too, Dale." When I hung up the phone, I felt so incredibly blessed. After all, the whole point of me being loving to my mom was not so that she would be more loving to me, yet this was what was happening. How could it be? Years of me demanding more and more from her and never getting enough … yet now that I had started to try to simply give, expecting nothing in return, I was getting what I had wanted all those years.

My sponsor simply told me, "Dale, you've been practicing the St. Francis Prayer and you didn't even know it. Keep on doing what you're doing." And I did.

Over the next 10 years, I practiced giving love to my mom, and we became very close. She shared with me about her childhood and early married life, and how she felt at different points in her life, and

I listened and began to understand why she reacted to certain things the way she did. I saw even more clearly that all the resentments I had held against her really had very little to do with me, and more to do with how she was raised and how she had been treated throughout her life. We actually became friends. The more I reached out to her in love, expecting nothing in return, the more she reached back to me in love.

We travelled together ... to New York City, Chicago, Paris, the south of France ... she came and visited me in Toronto every few months for a "girls' weekend" and we went to the opera, art galleries, films, the theatre, or just for a coffee on the Boardwalk.

I continued to pray whenever we spent time together. When we travelled together, I prayed even more. Every morning, I asked for my Higher Power to help me to put my ego aside and to give my mom the best day she could have.

Not all was "sweetness and light." We discovered that we were both control freaks, and we were both convinced that we were right and the other was wrong. But we were able to talk about it, laugh about it, and set some boundaries. And when one of us crossed one of the boundaries, we'd get a gentle reminder from the other. I can honestly say that my mom and I have not exchanged a harsh word in the last 10 years. Absolutely miraculous.

As I write this, my mom lies sleeping on the couch opposite me. She is dying. Six months ago, she was playing 18 holes of golf four times a week and was looking forward to one of our "girls' weekends." Then, a bit of congestion in her chest. A diagnosis of terminal lung cancer. No cure possible. Three weeks ago, her doctor told us that she would likely be gone within a month. So here I am, soaking up as much of her Spirit as I can, just watching her sleep.

I have been blessed to be able to spend a lot of time with my mom since her diagnosis, and I have been here for the last three weeks to help her die at home, as she wishes. It looks like it won't be much longer. She is skin and bone. I massage her daily. I bathe her, as she bathed me as a child. I get her oxygen. I listen to her talk about her death. I hold her as she cries. I sit with her silently, as she sleeps more and more, quietly slipping away. Each hour with her, just to be able to look at her as she sleeps, is more precious than the last.

There is nothing I need to say to my mom that hasn't been said. I am able to be completely present in each moment. Yes, my heart is breaking. But because a tiny bit of that St. Francis Prayer made its way into my soul, my breaking heart is full of my mom's Spirit. And for that, there are no words.

A Higher Purpose

Wayne M. (Punanai 2004)

My sobriety depends not upon a "Higher Power" but instead is based upon a "Higher Purpose."

I will explain that in a moment but first let me tell you a little about myself.

My problem with alcohol was bad — so bad that between 1992 and 2004, I was in four different rehabs.

After three months at Halton Recovery House, I managed to stay sober for a year and a half. I picked up a drink and the next thing I knew, I was in a psych ward. Years passed, and by 2004, I was jobless, homeless and friendless. Not even my brother would take a phone call from me.

It was then that I decided that I did not want to die a drunk. I knew I needed treatment to get started — again. In November 2004, I entered Renascent and completed treatment. My sobriety date is September 30, 2004.

Now, my higher purpose.

In the last two rehabs, I discovered that I was self-obsessed, with no concern for other people. It was brutal and fatal, unless I took action. My higher purpose is about as simple as I can make it (which is no small feat for an alcoholic). It is simply to be there and to participate in the human race. Even if I can't do anything to help, I need to be there if someone needs me. If I am using, I am not there for myself, let alone anyone else. This obviously requires I interact with others. I strongly believe that isolation in its many forms is one of the primary reasons we use and especially why we relapse.

I acknowledge that I am dependent on others for my sobriety. I must be a part of the human race. To do that on an ongoing basis, I must always endeavour to do the right thing.

AA was — and continues to be — my first line of defence against isolation. I know I can be honest and talk about real things in that environment. AA is not the only place where I can relate to others but it was a start. I know I also have people in my life outside of AA. Now I am a part of, not apart from. So now that I am a part of the human race, how do I act and what do I do in this strange arena of the real world?

I believe we can't think our way into good behaviour but we can behave our way into good thinking. What is good behaviour? It is doing the next right thing regardless of what I may feel like or think. This can be where the second use I make of AA can come in. For me the Steps are signposts and guides on how to behave as a normal human being. They also act like idiot lights on my dashboard of life. If in a certain situation one of those Steps keeps popping into my head, I know I need to look at something I am doing. For example, if I become resentful or angry, I need to look at what my part is in this (Step Four), and if I am wrong, I need to apologize and try to make it right (Step Ten).

After being sober for more than a year, I started volunteering at Renascent.

As time went by and because I always showed up and did well at what they gave me, they started offering me paid shifts. I was offered a full time job in 2007. It was to assess people who wanted to attend our treatment program. My job was to interview them and determine if they were a fit for us and, more importantly, if we were a fit for them.

To say I loved it would be the understatement of all time. For the first time in my life, I had a job that was not a job. You see, it was an ideal way for me to live my higher purpose. That way, I could be a useful part of the human race.

Everything at my job was going more than well until 2010 when I checked myself into the hospital with crippling stomach pain. Operations (two within a week) found colon cancer, which was removed.

No reprieve however. In February 2014, I was diagnosed with lung cancer, for which there is no cure (only, hopefully, control). Since then, I have gone through radiation therapy and three rounds of chemo. I recently started the fourth round. I have had thoughts of, and even discussions about, going back to work. No one knows just how much I miss it. You see, this work is all about my higher purpose.

I can remember the first time I mentioned this higher purpose when I spoke at a meeting. I was surprised at how many people came to me afterwards wanting to know more. This is still my core belief — the concept of others, not you.

Way back in 2004, in a psych ward, I decided I did not want to die a drunk.

And I won't.

Because I have a higher purpose.

Editor's Note: Wayne M. passed away on March 21, 2014. As he had resolved, he did not die a drunk; he died a clean and sober man who was wanted, needed and loved.

About Renascent

Over the last 45 years, Renascent has helped more than 45,000 Canadians find hope and healing in recovery from addiction.

The Renascent Fellowship was founded in 1970 by Paul J. Sullivan and a group of businessmen, half of whom were recovering alcoholics, with the goal of opening a new type of treatment centre. Renascent's centre would be a 12-step, abstinence-based and gender-specific drug and alcohol recovery program.

On October 20, 1971, our first client, Donald, walked through the doors of Renascent. Tens of thousands of clients would follow him throughout the following decades.

The Renascent Foundation was incorporated in 1983 to enhance funding for the treatment of alcoholism and drug addiction and ensure that no one would be turned away for lack of funds. With the support of the Foundation, Renascent began to offer programs for families whose loved ones struggle with the illness of addiction.

Today, Renascent owns and operates four centres: the Paul J. Sullivan Centre for men in Brooklin, the Punanai Centre for men in Toronto, the Graham Munro Centre for women in Toronto, and the Lillian and Don Wright Family Health Centre in Toronto — home to our head office and family programs.

Still fiercely committed to 12-step, abstinence-based treatment, Renascent is changing the conversation about addiction and recovery in Canada. Renascent battles the family disease of alcoholism and drug addiction by helping the entire family, including kids. The largest residential treatment centre in Ontario, Renascent's treatment programs are trauma-informed and concurrent-capable; relapse prevention and family care services are available over the phone to ensure distance is never a barrier. Renascent was fully accredited in 2014, meeting standards of excellence assessed by external, non-biased reviewers.

Renascent offers immediate and affordable access to treatment within 24 hours. Donors, working together with our provincial funding partner (Toronto Central LHIN), safeguard public access for the 80% of Canadians who cannot afford treatment. At Renascent, we are passionate about the promise of recovery and we believe that recovery must be available for all who seek it.

24/7 Recovery Helpline: 1-866-232-1212

www.renascent.ca

Renascent
The road to recovery starts here.